Becoming One

Intimacy in Marriage

Becoming One

Intimacy in Marriage

Robert F. Stahmann, Ph.D.
Wayne R. Young, M.D.
Julie G. Grover, M.D.

Covenant

Covenant Communications, Inc.

Cover image © digital Vision/Getty Images
Cover design copyrighted 2004 by Covenant Communications, Inc.
Published by Covenant Communications, Inc.
American Fork, Utah

Printed in Canada
First Printing: June 2004

12 11 10 09 08 07 06 05 04   10 9 8 7 6 5 4 3 2 1

ISBN 1-59156-414-X

Dedication

We dedicate this book with appreciation, love, and affection to our spouses and eternal companions: Kathy Stahmann, Carol Young, and Keith Grover.

Acknowledgments

We acknowledge the contributions of many unnamed persons involved in our professional lives who have directly and indirectly contributed to this book. We thank patients, clients, students, and colleagues who have provided examples, insight, and information which have shaped our thinking and writing. Particular thanks are expressed to Shauna Humphreys, Managing Editor at Covenant Communications, Inc. and to Lisa McMullin for their exemplary editorial work. They shaped our best writing efforts into a book that even more clearly conveys the information and ideas that we desired to communicate.

Table of Contents

Introduction

Congratulations! Whether you've recently married or are planning a wedding soon, or even if you have been married for several years, this is a wonderful and exciting time in your lives. And we are certain you are determined to make your marriage great in every way you can. Physical and sexual intimacy are important parts of the marriage you are building. Sexuality in marriage is a sacred bond that can bind husband and wife together and bring great joy into their lives. Unfortunately, problems and conflict over the sexual aspects of marriage can also contribute to unhappiness in marriage and are a major cause of divorce. We believe many of these sexual difficulties can be prevented by starting a marriage with a healthy sexual relationship based on open communication, unselfishness, and love. Establishing such a relationship requires effort, patience, and a knowledge and understanding of the sexual and physical aspects of human intimacies.

As counselors and physicians, couples often ask us questions regarding physical intimacy. We have found very few sources available that are written from an LDS perspective. This book is written to give you a perspective of how you and your marriage partner are similar and, at the same time, different in your physical, sexual, and emotional makeup. The first 10 chapters deal primarily with the sexual aspect of your relationship. However we haven't ignored the other aspects like the emotional, social, spiritual, and intellectual that complete a marriage. In fact, we mention them often, but we mention them in their sexual context—how they affect your sexual relationship. The last two chapters change focus just a bit. All aspects of marriage—emotional, spiritual, intellectual, and sexual—are given equal time. We talk about how couples can learn more about each other, learn how to keep their marriage alive, and learn why it's important to open up and talk with each other about basic human emotions and needs.

You may ask yourselves why we devoted ten chapters to sex and only two to everything else. It is because our experience has been that when people think or talk about such sensitive topics as human emotions and sexuality, they become uncomfortable and even confused. And both of you have expectations. As you talk with each other about intimate emotions and sexuality, you'll find your opinions and expectations are not exactly the same. You need to communicate your feelings and expectations to your partner in order to enhance your understanding of him or her.

In this book we're taking on the role of premarital and marital counselors and are giving you permission to read about and discuss intimate physical and emotional aspects of your relationship. Sexually conservative people may feel they need permission to openly discuss these things. Before your engagement, it was appropriate to shy away from discussing sexuality. However, now that you are approaching marriage, or are already married, it is not only appropriate, but essential for you to discuss this topic.

Our goal is to provide adequate, accurate, and appropriate information about human sexuality and intimacy within the sacred bonds of marriage. In this book we make specific suggestions and share candid advice that many couples have found useful. However, just as with all advice, you need to evaluate it and decide together what is useful for you. We hope you will creatively adapt this information to your unique relationship. Most importantly we hope that reading this book will generate open and honest discussions about intimacy and sexuality.

However, this book is not intended to solve serious medical or sexual problems. For these issues, we advise consultation and treatment from a professional. After reading this book, we hope you will feel more comfortable seeking professional help for specific problems.

One Caution

If you are not yet married, we strongly encourage both of you to read and study this information separately, prior to your wedding night. On the other hand, we recommend that you prayerfully consider which portions of this book to read and study together. As a couple you should discuss the topic of family planning (chapter nine) before your wedding, and dialogue about the many dimensions of your relationship (chapters eleven and twelve). Depending on your level of comfort and your level of knowledge, you may want to discuss other portions of the book. We recommend that you do not discuss the detailed portions of chapters three through seven before your wedding. Also, if at any time during your study of this book you find yourselves becoming sexually aroused, you should stop reading and move to a more public place.

If questions arise regarding material contained in this manual, you should ask someone with whom you feel comfortable and who is also knowledgeable about such matters. Such persons as your parent of the same sex or your physician might be helpful. They may be able to sensitively discuss your questions and may also be aware of other information or ideas that can be helpful to you.

We recommend you take this book along on your honeymoon, since this is a great time for you as newlyweds to read and discuss it together. If you're currently married, we recommend that you read and study this material together. Doing so will help open channels of communication that will help you better understand each other's physical, sexual, and emotional needs. In addition, learning and practicing sex together can be fun, exciting, and extremely rewarding.

Robert F. Stahmann, Ph.D.
Wayne R. Young, M.D.
Julie G. Grover, M.D.

Chapter One

Marriage Is a Celebration

So you're getting married! Or, perhaps you've recently married. In either case, the two of you are attempting to build the best marriage that anyone can have. Excitement, commitment, love, and dreams for the future occupy your mind and heart. How wonderful that the two of you have found each other—the person you want as your companion for this life and for eternity.

The story of how you met, your dating and courtship experiences, and your decision to marry are very exciting. Recall the weeks and months during which you got to know each other and moved toward the commitment to marry. Such things as mutual attraction, shared interests and activities, friendship, compatibility, common values, religious faith, emotional closeness, good communication, attitudes toward money and material things, and spiritual experiences led you to the decision to wed. Marriage is a celebration of all that and more!

Marriage Is a Multidimensional Process

In this book we want you to think of marriage as a process that begins before the wedding and continues after it. Your wedding is, or was, the legal ceremony that celebrates and sanctions the marriage. It is just one event, joyous as it is, that takes place during the marriage process. The complete process of marriage is wonderfully complex, with many different dimensions. Let us show you what we mean by the dimensions of marriage.

- *Social.* Your marriage has a social dimension in which the two of you enjoy doing things together and look forward to spending time together. A measure of happiness and humor comes from expectations, experiences, and traditions that are a part of your unique experiences.

- *Emotional.* This dimension is the ability and desire to share personal feelings, to trust and be trusted, and to feel safe and secure with each other.

- *Cognitive.* Marriage has a cognitive and planning dimension, which includes sharing thoughts about life, as well as making plans, discussing goals, and carving out your future together.

- *Financial.* This fiscal dimension deals with your decisions concerning how you will earn and spend money, and how you will manage your temporal resources.

- *Spiritual.* Marriage has a spiritual and philosophical dimension that includes sharing spiritual and religious attitudes, behaviors, and life experiences.

- *Intergenerational.* This particular dimension links you to your families-of-origin and to extended family relationships.

- *Affectional.* Marriage has an affectional dimension in which you nurture and support each other emotionally and physically, but in nonsexual ways.

- *Sexual.* The sexual dimension is one in which you share your love for each other by sharing your bodies and physically becoming one.

All of these dimensions, except for the sexual dimension, are developing during dating and courtship. During that particular time, the marriage tapestry is already being woven and patterns begin to emerge. Those patterns will continue throughout your marriage.

Make those patterns as beautiful and harmonious as possible. And after your wedding, when you add the sexual dimension, let it only add beauty to your marriage tapestry.

The Joy of Marriage

It has been said that "Latter-day Saints have an exceptionally positive view of procreation. . . . The divine plan of procreation provides physical bodies for premortal spirits. Thus, 'children are an heritage of the Lord' (Ps. 127:3). To beget and bear children is central to God's plan for the development of his children on earth. The powers of procreation therefore are of divine origin."[1]

The Bible says it isn't good for man to be alone. When Adam and Eve were placed in the Garden of Eden, they were taught, "Therefore shall a man leave his father and his mother, and shall cleave unto his wife; and they shall be one flesh. And they were both naked, the man and his wife, and were not ashamed" (Moses 3:24–25). Every couple has the opportunity to fill the measure of their creation and find joy in doing so. In other words, "Live joyfully with the wife whom thou lovest" (Eccl. 9:9).

President Spencer W. Kimball has told us that "While marriage is difficult, and discordant and frustrated marriages are common, yet real, lasting happiness is possible, and marriage can be more an exultant ecstasy that the human mind can conceive. This is within the reach of every couple, every person."[2] What a wonderful promise and goal for every married couple! Recent studies have shown that individuals who are married live longer, are healthier, possess more wealth and economic assets, feel more fulfilled in their lives, have happier and more successful children, and have a more satisfying sexual relationship than their counterparts who are single or cohabiting.[3] Marriage requires effort if it is to grow and become mutually lasting, satisfying, and fulfilling. But the benefits are worth the effort.

A loving and joyful marriage is one in which both partners are sexually fulfilled and nurtured. The sexual relationship is one of the most important aspects of marriage. It keeps a marriage vital. President Kimball stated, "The Bible celebrates sex and its proper use, presenting it as God-created, God-ordained, God-blessed. It makes it plain that God himself implanted the physical magnetism between the sexes for two reasons: for the propagation of the human race, and for the expression of the kind of love between man and wife that makes for true oneness. His command to the first man and woman to be 'one flesh' was as important as his command to 'be fruitful and multiply.'"[4]

While sensual feelings and sexual activity are truly a gift to men and women from their Maker, scripture and modern revelation clearly teach that sexual relations should occur only within the bonds of marriage. "Thou shalt love thy wife with all thy heart, and shalt cleave unto her and none else" (D&C 42:22). Sexuality in marriage is a sacred bond.

Trust Results from Premarital Chastity

When complete trust exists between partners, the strongest emotional and sexual relationship occurs. Trust in and for each other is one of the single most important factors for holding a relationship together. It allows each partner to feel safe and secure. Sexual intercourse prior to marriage can result in having less trust in each other after the wedding.

When couples make a commitment to control their sexual appetites, desires, and passions until they are married, trust for each other will increase significantly. With increased trust comes an increased security in the relationship. This increased trust and security helps couples weather the emotional, physical, financial, and other challenges that every marriage encounters.

It is our strong belief that, aside from religious reasons, waiting for marriage to begin a sexual relationship makes good sense. There is a wonderful power in knowing that you have been able to live your values and that you can thereby trust yourself, your partner, and your relationship.

Repentance and Forgiveness

While ideally both partners will have remained chaste prior to marriage, we understand that in reality this may not be the case. Fortunately, our Heavenly Father's plan allows individuals to repent and be forgiven. For those who have truly repented, Heavenly Father remembers their sins no more. We should do the same.

If a past indiscretion has been repented of and forgiven, it should remain in the past and have no relevance to the current relationship. As a couple, you should go forward as if it never occurred. The plan of repentance allows you to build your marriage around current mutual trust and fidelity.

Maintaining Chastity Before Marriage

It is true that as a relationship becomes more intimate, couples may have increased struggles in maintaining control of their physical relationship. Yet, in a caring and loving relationship, couples have the power to control physical behaviors so that they do not violate their sexual standards. Some ideas that couples have found helpful in maintaining chastity include:

- Discuss together the fact that you want to maintain chastity before the wedding. Share your personal feelings about the importance of this with each other. There is a tremendous power in expressing your beliefs verbally, because as you understand each other's feelings, you will find that you will work to respect and honor those feelings.

- Together, set limits on your physical and affectional behavior. What is permissible in regard to kissing, touching, and displays of affection? Be specific with each other.

- Establish the "rule" that either partner can, and will, call for a "stop" to affection if he or she feels that it is going too far. Then stop immediately. Respect it.

- Plan so that you will not get into situations or settings that might lead to affectional or sexual problems. Consider such actions as setting your own curfews, spending most of your time as a couple in public or with others rather than alone, etc.

- Meet regularly with one or both of your bishops to receive counsel and advice on marriage and family life. If possible, also spend time with each other's families for the same reasons.

SEXUAL FIDELITY AFTER MARRIAGE

After marriage, a strong, monogamous relationship between partners who are sexually faithful to each other provides a safe harbor. This security plays a key role in rejuvenating both partners for the everyday world outside their marriage. A safe harbor is one in which both partners feel secure, loved physically, and cherished emotionally and sexually. This security is the result of commitment, which began with both partners having been morally clean and chaste before the marriage. When a partner is unfaithful, the trust is violated. Infidelity strikes the relationship a serious and, oftentimes, fatal blow.

Trust and emotional support are destroyed if a spouse is unfaithful. This is true for both women and men. If wives and husbands cannot trust their partners not to hurt them again, they will hold back in the bedroom and in the relationship. They may try, but will be unable to relax and let go. This can make it impossible to enjoy a mutually satisfying sexual relationship.

Dr. David Mace, who is a longtime marriage counselor and writer, spent his career observing the dynamics of marriage. He pointed out that "the sexual side of marriage is closely linked with the emotional and personal elements in the relationship . . . What the married couple have to achieve, therefore, is a sexual relationship that expresses, sustains, and renews their deepest and most tender feelings for each other."[5]

IMPORTANCE OF THE SEXUAL RELATIONSHIP WITHIN THE BONDS OF MARRIAGE

Within the bonds of marriage, sexual relationships are not only all right, but are an important means of nurturing your relationship, which allows you to grow together. For you as a married couple, sexual feelings and actions are righteous and good and should be shared. Even in the Bible it says, "Rejoice with the wife of thy youth . . . let her breasts satisfy thee at all times; and be thou ravished always with her love (Prov. 5:18–19)." President Spencer W. Kimball said, "The Bible makes plain that evil, when related to sex means not the use of something inherently corrupt but the misuse of something pure and good. It teaches clearly that sex can be a wonderful servant but a terrible master: that it can be a creative force more powerful than any other in the fostering of a love, companionship, happiness or can be the most destructive of all life's forces."[6]

When you as a married couple unite in the act of sexual love, it's an exclusively intimate union shared only with each other. It's the single physical act that provides bonding, uniting, and enrichment, which are vitally important to your marriage.

The Apostle Paul said, "Let every man have his own wife, and let every woman have her own husband. Let the husband render unto the wife due benevolence: and likewise also the wife unto the husband. The wife hath not power of her own body, but the husband: and likewise also the husband hath not power of his own body, but the wife" (1 Cor. 7:2–4). In this context Paul is giving advice to married couples regarding how important it is for them to attend to each other's emotional and sexual needs.

"Depart ye not one from the other, except it be with consent for a time, that ye may give yourselves to fasting and prayer; and come together again, that Satan tempt you not for your incontinency" (JST, 1 Cor. 7:5). In other words, you shouldn't withhold sex from each other without both of you understanding the reason, e.g., illness or fatigue; and have that be only temporary. Otherwise, as this scripture indicates, Satan could tempt you, which, (among other things) can create conflict or disharmony in your marriage. As a married couple, you should strive to communicate openly and learn to satisfy each other both emotionally and sexually. In a strong and loving relationship there should be no coercion or neglect, no pressure or vindictive withholding.

Without a doubt, sexual intimacy can bring you closer or push you apart. You can be functioning well in everything else, but if one or both of you are unhappy in your affectional and sexual relationship, you can be quite unhappy in your marriage. But a good sexual relationship, kept within the proper boundaries, will help keep your marriage strong and will improve many aspects of your marriage. It will help you reduce the importance of the other problems you face. It will help bind you together such that you can surmount other life challenges as a team. Being able to give and receive physical pleasure allows both of you to develop the closeness and intimacy necessary to become one in both heart and purpose.

Note that while your relationship must be strong and secure even before sex can be fully enjoyed, expressing love through sex can dramatically increase your love for each other. For example, a wife's (or husband's) openness to having sex will often increase her husband's love for her and vice versa. Even when one of you feels cool toward the other, being sexual and feeling love for each other during this intimate time will often help you open up and assist in reestablishing emotional closeness.

Studies show that a positive sexual relationship between a husband and wife increases their attraction for each other, stimulates greater energy, and promotes better health.[7] Additionally (as Paul noted in the scriptures), a strong sexual bond between a husband and wife is a powerful resource for resisting temptation. In short, a loving and enjoyable sexual relationship is God's special reward to those who work hard to make the expression of physical love a priority in their lives.

We emphasize here that what you and you spouse consider to be a loving and enjoyable sexual relationship is for you two to determine. Don't be influenced by media or other sources of what your sexual relationship "should be." The process of defining and discovering this for yourselves is one of the joys of marriage. There will be frustrations and misunderstandings, but that is normal. Communication, love, respect, and caring are all important as you develop nurturing sexuality in your marriage.

Marriage is a living entity. Marriage is an eternal process. If a marriage is cultivated and nourished, it will thrive. If it's neglected, it will wither and die. Sexual relations in marriage are the same. Just as playing the piano requires time and attention, so does developing the ability to give and accept sexual pleasure in marriage. Most important, great sex isn't the result of a passionate marriage; it's one of the most important ways to create passion in marriage. Don't be impatient in achieving this in your marriage. Knowing and appreciating the physical, sexual, and emotional differences (and similarities) between you and your partner is essential if you wish to have a strong and healthy marriage based on love and understanding.

Chapter Two

Human Intimacy

Intimacy is expressed in many forms, most of which are nonsexual. Intimacy begins when social, spiritual, emotional, and intellectual experiences are shared: religious activities, social events, leisure activities, sports, talking, and even eating. As your relationship with your partner developed, you probably became intimate doing most of these things. This was appropriate and necessary for a relationship to be meaningful to both of you.

An intimate relationship is one of caring, mutual trust, and acceptance. Caring is showing genuine concern for the person's well-being. Mutual trust is the feeling that you will not be harmed or hurt by the other. Acceptance is recognition or approval of each other. A relationship with these qualities sets the foundation for healthy sexual intimacy. Though this book primarily addresses physical affection and sexual intimacy, keep in mind that all the other forms of intimacy are crucial in maintaining a well-functioning relationship. They are indeed the basis for healthy physical affection and sexual intimacy.

The Meaning of Physical Affection to Men and Women

Both men and women have the basic need to be intimate and close with another person. Yet, what this means from both a sexual and emotional standpoint is different for men and women. This chapter, while somewhat generalized, will help both men and women understand some of their basic differences regarding intimacy. Having a basic understanding of these differences is important so that misunderstanding, frustrations, and anger can be avoided. Being aware of, and understanding, these important differences is necessary if you are to continue to develop a strong and loving relationship in your marriage.

It's been said that, typically, men give love and commitment in order get physical affection and sex. Women give physical affection and sex in order to get commitment and love. It might also be said that men typically hunger for sex while women hunger for romance. Men initially give and receive love to fulfill their physical needs, while women initially give and receive love to fulfill their emotional needs. While these statements may sound like stereotypes, and of course not all relationships are so black and white, we have found that for most couples, there is at least some element of truth in these generalizations.

Especially for newlyweds, it's not often that women say, "He's just a cold fish, never responsive to me sexually when I'm in the mood. All he wants to do is cuddle. He hardly has any sexual drive or interest. It must be his hormones." Conversely, seldom do new grooms complain, "She's just an animal. All she wants is sex, sex, sex. She's just interested in my body. After we've made love, she just rolls over and falls asleep." Neither husbands nor wives will have these complaints about their partners if they understand their spouse's physical and emotional needs.

Men and women generally have different motivations for seeking sexual intimacy. Men commonly have a stronger or more constant spontaneous sexual drive or interest. Women certainly have this inherent sexual drive, especially early on in a relationship, at certain times of their menstrual cycle, or after a period of separation. But more often women seek sexual intimacy for reasons more closely related to emotional and other types of intimacy: to gain a greater closeness to their spouse, to show love, commitment, and tenderness.

As emotional intimacy with her spouse increases, a woman has a greater desire for sexual intimacy, is more responsive to her husband, and generally enjoys sex more. A pleasurable sexual experience then also makes her feel more emotionally close to her husband. Emotional and sexual intimacy are so closely intertwined that a woman cannot be fulfilled sexually if she is not fulfilled emotionally.

We believe that most husbands wouldn't have to talk their wives into sexual relations if they would provide what their wives long for most: emotional intimacy in the areas of trust, tenderness, caring, acceptance, and good communication. Women need to feel loved and nurtured before they begin to be aroused and develop desires for sexual intimacy. For women, emotional intimacy is at least as important as the act of having sex.

While women need to feel loved before they can become sexually aroused, men often need to be sexually aroused before they can truly feel loved. It's through sexual activity that men are emotionally and physically fulfilled. It's through a loving sexual relationship that their hearts are opened and they're able to express their love to their wives. Sex allows men to become aware of their wives' need for love and emotional support. Unless partners understand this basic difference between men and women, it will be difficult for them to find a common ground so that the emotional and physical needs of both are fulfilled.

When women find themselves losing interest in sex, it's most often not a problem with their hormones. Instead, it's often because their husbands haven't met their emotional and affectional needs. If a husband seeks to fulfill his sexual appetites first, his wife will be left unsatisfied and less inclined in the future to meet his needs. A man needs to learn to be sensitive to and take care of his wife's emotional needs before seeking his own physical and sexual satisfaction. Then, as his wife's emotional needs are fulfilled, both partners will become interested in taking care of each other's needs. The husband who satisfies his wife's emotional needs first, and who then pays attention to her sexual desires, will find his own needs satisfied too.

Understanding each other's feelings is the key. When couples understand their own feelings as well as the feelings of their spouse, 70 to 80 percent of the time that is all that is needed. When understanding or agreement are not reached, there are communication skills and problem-solving techniques that can be used. The important thing to remember is that if communication is a problem, like any skill, it can be improved.

IS DISAGREEMENT OR CONFLICT SERIOUS?

No, in fact all married couples will have some disagreement or conflict. It's normal to disagree in some things. Two heads are better than one—actually making healthy disagreement a valuable step in decision making. Disagreements can even be used to move a relationship forward. In fact, it's been said that a good marriage has three "C's." Commitment to the marriage and to each other, effective Communication, and the ability to use Conflict to improve the relationship. To properly use conflict is a sign that differences can be worked out. Often differences in opinions lead to better solutions or ideas than either of the two original points of view! However, if bickering and fighting frequently occur and solutions seem difficult to come by due to the emotions generated by the situation, then such disagreements and conflicts can damage the relationship. You may benefit from consulting with your bishop or a professional to help you work through these problems. Putting your heads in the sand and ignoring the signs of dissatisfaction and unhappiness may lead to much more serious problems.

Chapter Three

Your Bodies and How They Work

In our culture, there are vast differences in what young people learn about the anatomy and physiology of men and women as related to sexuality. Often young adults approach marriage with inadequate knowledge of their own or their partner's body. This can lead to misunderstandings or unnecessary anxiety. The following section reviews basic anatomy (structures) and physiology (how they function). For more information, and diagrams of male and female anatomy, see:

http://training.seer.cancer.gov/module_anatomy/unit12_1_repdt_intro.html

These are internet resources that provide drawings of male and female internal and external anatomy of the genitalia.

Early Development

As you probably know, the gender of a child is determined at the time of conception when the sperm meets the egg to form an embryo. In the human embryo, there are no physical differences between the male and female embryo until about the twelfth week. At that time the male embryo begins to produce certain hormones and proteins that are not produced by the female. Therefore, all the parts that become male are also found in the female. Corresponding parts in the male and female are called homologous structures. Thus, homologous structures are the glans or head of the male penis and the female clitoris; the male scrotum and female vaginal lips or labia; and the male foreskin and female clitoral hood.

FEMALE ANATOMY

Vulva is the collective name for the external female parts. The outer folds (or outer lips) are called the labia majora and correspond to the male scrotum. The inner folds (or inner lips) are called the labia minora and correspond to the part of the male penis that surrounds the urethra (the tube that goes to the bladder). The clitoris is located just above the vagina and the urethra. It is covered in front by part of the labia minora. The skin covering the clitoris is called the clitoral hood. Just as the penis is the most sensitive part of a man's sexual organs, the clitoris is the most sensitive part for a woman. The clitoris becomes erect with stimulation just as the penis does. Stimulation of the clitoris is essential for a woman to experience her greatest sexual satisfaction.

The hymen is a membrane that partially covers the opening to the vagina. The diameter of the opening through the hymen varies in women, even for those who aren't sexually active. The hymen is partially dilated in most women before they become sexually active. Some women may need to do stretching exercises or even have minor surgery to enlarge the opening before their wedding (see chapter 4).

The vagina is the tube made up of thin, sensitive skin that runs from the vulva (opening to the outside) to the uterus. It is attached to the cervix, which is the lower portion of and opening to the uterus. The bladder is in front of the vagina and the rectum is behind it. The opening of the urethra (the short tube that runs from the bladder to the outside of the body) is located close to and just in front of the opening of the vagina and a little ways behind the clitoris. The location of the urethral opening is important because excessive contact with it can be uncomfortable and can also increase the risk of bladder infections.

MALE ANATOMY

The penis is made up of three columns of spongy erectile tissue. The glans, or head of the penis, is the most sensitive part. At birth the glans is completely covered with tissue called foreskin. Circumcision is a procedure where this foreskin is removed, usually just after birth. Although there is no compelling medical reason to perform a circumcision, many male infants are circumcised at birth for religious reasons or, more often, because it is customary in our society.

Testes are contained in the scrotum. The testes produce both sperm and testosterone. For sperm to be viable, it must be produced at a temperature lower than normal body temperature.

Erogenous Zones

The erogenous zones are the commonly considered sexually sensitive areas of your body. For example, the breasts, penis, vagina, and clitoris are some erogenous areas. However, many professionals who deal with human sexuality state that for both males and females, the whole body can be sexually aroused. That's why nothing more than kissing can be very arousing to most men and women. One counselor we know states that the largest sex organ is actually the skin because caressing, stroking, and just touching naked skin can be arousing to most men and women. However, there are areas of the body that are more sensitive than others. The two most sensitive centers of sexual sensation are the glans in the male and the nipples, breasts, and clitoris in the female. A sizable percentage of men report that nipples and breasts are sensitive areas for them as well.

Female Sexual Arousal

The complex nature of women's sexual organs makes it possible for their physical and emotional response to sexual stimulation to be much deeper and longer lasting than it is for men. The tissue around the opening of the vagina becomes engorged with blood (like the penis becomes erect in men), resulting in the labia minora swelling to two or three times their normal size. Glands surrounding the opening of the vagina begin to secrete fluid so that the vagina and vulva (labia minora, majora, and the opening of the vagina) also become wet. The clitoris may or may not increase in size and the vagina increases in length.

Drs. William Masters and Virginia Johnson, pioneers in the field of sex research and therapy, conducted extensive research that shows that females experience only one type of orgasm that begins with the clitoris and increases with stimulation until orgasm is finally felt throughout the pelvis. They report that for women to achieve orgasm, clitoral stimulation must take place, either directly or indirectly. In fact 60 percent of all women require direct manual stimulation.[8]

MALE SEXUAL AROUSAL

As men become aroused, a narrowing of the veins in the penis causes a decrease in the amount of blood that leaves the penis to return to the heart. As the penis becomes engorged with blood it becomes erect. A sterile lubricant is secreted from the Cowper's gland into the urethra during early arousal. This fluid allows for easier passage of sperm through the urethra and may help decrease the acidic environment of the urethra, thereby increasing the likelihood that more sperm will survive for fertilizing the egg. At times, some of this fluid may leak onto the head of the penis. It is important to note that a small amount of sperm is also contained in this fluid that is released early during sexual excitement. This release of fluid makes it possible to impregnate the female even when the man withdraws from her vagina prior to ejaculating.

As the shaft of the penis is stimulated, sexual excitement builds until inevitable rhythmic contractions occur in the muscles surrounding the prostate and urethra, which propel the sperm out of the penis. This is called ejaculation. The narrowing of the blood vessels in the penis then ceases, allowing the trapped blood to return to the heart, and the penis once again becomes soft.

THE SEXUAL RESPONSE CYCLE

Research in sexual functioning has provided information to lay to rest many myths that previously existed regarding human sexual arousal and response. Four specific phases in the human sexual-response cycle have been identified by Masters and Johnson that can help us understand how the body functions physically. (We will discuss the psychological response in chapters 5 and 6.) The four physical phases of the sexual-response cycle are:

1. Excitement or Arousal
2. Plateau (Foreplay)
3. Climax or Orgasm
4. Resolution

The excitement phase begins when a sensory event or thought stimulates the nerves and hormones. Blood rushes to the pelvic area for both males and females. In the male, the blood causes the penis to become erect; in the female it causes a fluid to be secreted from glands just outside the vagina, as well as from the vaginal walls. Her vulva becomes wet. After fifteen to sixty seconds, the male becomes fully aroused with an erection. For the female, full arousal of her sexual organs requires considerably more time. There is a gradual buildup of sexual excitement for both men and women as respiration, heart rate, and blood pressure increases.

The plateau phase of sexual response is often referred to as foreplay or love play. The length of this phase varies considerably. It begins with full arousal and ends with orgasm. Thus, depending on participants and the situation, the plateau phase may last a few minutes, or up to or even exceeding an hour. Simple caresses lead to penetration and rhythmic movement. During this phase, sexual excitement and feelings are at their maximum. As orgasm approaches, there's a feeling of impending, inevitable release, and movements become harder and faster. Women report a great desire to have their vagina filled and an increased desire for firmer pressure on their clitoris. Men report feeling like every muscle is tight awaiting the impending explosion.

The orgasm phase is the release of all the built-up excitement in an explosion of pleasure. Men ejaculate, and women experience rhythmic contractions of all of the muscles involving the pelvic area, which include muscles around both the vagina and vaginal opening.

The resolution phase begins after sexual climax or orgasm. Once a man climaxes, a refractory period occurs during which he's unable to become erect and climax again. This time period is highly variable between men, varying from minutes to hours depending on several factors, including the age of the man. As a man ages, the refractory period lengthens. Women, on the other hand, can continue to climax and experience subsequent orgasms that may even become progressively stronger than the previous ones.

Immediately after orgasm the blood leaves the pelvic region for both men and women, all the muscles relax, and a feeling of peace permeates the entire body. Heart rates, blood pressure, and respiration gradually return to normal. Men release a chemical in their brain that stimulates sleep. This same response is not seen in females.

Chapter Four

Medical and Practical Preparation for Marriage

The Premarital Exam

As a bride-to-be, you should have a complete physical examination, including a pelvic exam before your wedding. This exam can be performed by your family doctor, a gynecologist, or a nurse practitioner or physician's assistant with experience in women's health. Especially if you have never had a pelvic exam before, but even if you have, it's important to make sure your body is ready for the new physical relationship you are entering. Your doctor will probably ask you general questions about your health and perform a general physical examination prior to performing a pelvic exam.

The pelvic exam is often a source of great anxiety for young women, especially those who have not been sexually active before. However, if done carefully and sensitively, a pelvic exam should not be painful and usually involves only minor (if any) discomfort. The doctor should first examine the outside anatomy (the vulva). He or she should then examine the hymen, which is the band of tissue surrounding the opening to the vagina. In a female baby before birth, the hymen completely closes off the opening to the vagina, but by birth the hymen mostly dissolves. There is great variation in how completely this tissue dissolves. In some women there is very little of the hymen left by adulthood, and in others the hymen is almost completely intact. If the hymen is too tight it may need stretching prior to the wedding night. If this is the case, your doctor may recommend using either a cone-shaped plastic dilator or your fingers to stretch the tight tissue for a few minutes each day. Occasionally minor surgery may be required to enlarge the opening. For these reasons, it is recommended that your exam be performed at least two to three months prior to the wedding.

The next part of the exam is usually the speculum exam. A speculum is an instrument the doctor places in the vagina to hold it slightly open so that he or she can examine the inside of the vagina and the cervix, which is the opening of the uterus into the vagina. Your doctor may or may not do a pap smear at this point. A pap smear is a specific test that is often, but not always, done at the time of a pelvic exam. Your doctor will gently brush the surface of the cervix to get a sample of the skinlike cells that cover the cervix so they can be examined under a microscope. A pap smear is a screening test for cervical cancer, which is curable if found in the early or precancerous stages.

After the speculum examination the doctor will probably perform a bimanual examination in which one or two fingers are placed in your vagina and one hand presses on your lower abdomen. This allows your doctor to feel your uterus and ovaries to be certain they are normal in size and shape.

Before or after your physical examination your doctor should discuss the advantages and disadvantages of different family planning methods and help you decide which is best for you. (See chapter 9 for information that will help you be more prepared for this discussion.) He or she may also give you limited information regarding sexuality and the physical and emotional differences between men and women. You should feel free to ask any questions regarding these issues. Your fiancé may come for the discussion portion of your visit if you are both comfortable with this. If not, you should discuss these issues, including birth control, together at a later time. If there is not time for detailed discussion or counseling at your premarital visit, you may want to arrange a second visit or seek other sources of information (friends, family, the Internet, books, a counselor, etc.).

In addition to the premarital exam, a postwedding follow-up may be helpful to answer your questions and address concerns that may have occurred to you after your wedding.

Pelvic Floor Muscles

At some point in the pelvic exam, you will probably be asked to relax your pelvic floor muscles. These are strong muscles which run from your pubic bone in front to your tailbone in back. They surround the openings of your urethra, vagina, and rectum, and when contracted, they tighten these openings. Many women are not aware of these muscles, but with practice you can learn to contract and relax these muscles. Practicing contraction of your pelvic floor muscles is termed Kegel exercises. Your doctor may ask you to contract these muscles during your pelvic examination. When first learning to do Kegel exercises, practice stopping your stream while urinating and then relaxing and contracting to let only a small amount of urine out at a time. You can also try placing two fingers inside your vagina and contracting the muscles to squeeze your fingers.

Kegel exercises were first used to improve the muscular tone of the pelvic floor to decrease urinary incontinence in women. However, women who were doing these exercises for urinary control found it also improved their sexual pleasure as well as their ability to achieve orgasm. Learning to relax your pelvic floor muscles will help allow for more comfortable intercourse the first few times. Strengthening these muscles may improve your sexual functioning and enjoyment.

We recommend that you begin Kegel exercises several weeks to months before your wedding. Start with ten contractions three times a day. Slowly contract the muscles, hold each contraction for six seconds, then slowly relax. Gradually increase the number of contractions to twenty or thirty contractions three to six times per day. You can do these exercises while waiting at a red light, watching TV, waiting in line, before you get out of bed in the morning, or at almost any other time.

Premarital Counseling

Most people say that premarital counseling or education is very helpful before marriage. Couples who didn't have the chance to participate in premarital education or counseling tell us that they would have done so if it had been available. Premarital counseling or education is a process designed to enhance and enrich relationships and make marriages more satisfactory and stable. Premarital counseling provides information and insights in areas such as finances, affection, sexuality, family relationships, marital goals, and roles. Topics and ideas for couples to discuss are presented and reading materials suggested to strengthen knowledge and skills in areas such as communication, problem solving, decision making, conflict resolution, and other such things. A premarital inventory, such as RELATE (see chapter 11), is often taken by the couple to give them insights and information about themselves and their relationship. Often LDS stakes or wards have such programs or offer firesides dealing with marriage preparation. The local office of LDS Family Services is another resource that may list specific programs in your geographical area. Web sites such as www.familylife.byu.edu; www.beforeforever.byu.edu; and www.relate-institute.com contain information and links to other sources. An excellent site regarding marriage preparation and enhancement is www.smartmarriages.com. Seeking or participating in premarital counseling is a sign of strength, not weakness. It strengthens your desire to have the best possible marriage.

IS A HONEYMOON IMPORTANT?

Yes! After the wedding, we recommend that the newlyweds plan at least one week to relax and become intimately acquainted beyond what they were able to do during the time they were engaged. While going to interesting and exotic places is a wonderful way to do this, it is not required. Some couples may find it less stressful to have few planned activities and to find a retreat close (but not too close) to home to avoid long travel times. What is important is that you are alone together and are able to focus only on each other. Having a magnificent time together is important, but the most important aspect of your honeymoon is having time to become better acquainted with each other both from a physical and emotional standpoint.

You now don't have to limit yourselves at all in your show of affection and love. Basking in the love of each other's arms and looking into each other's eyes will, in many respects, set the tenor of your lives together forever. Don't fill your itinerary so full of activities that you don't have enough time alone together in the privacy of your hotel room. Have fun! But most important, please understand that it is not necessary (or possible) to resolve all of your sexual adjustments to each other's needs during the week or two of your honeymoon. That will take some time. When you get down the road several years, you won't remember how great sex was during that time. Instead you'll remember the sandy, white beaches, the sunsets, the exotic restaurants, and beautiful scenery. And you will remember how much you were in love with each other.

Husbands, by your attitude and behavior, don't make your wife think she now has to become your sex slave. The more restraint you can exercise during your honeymoon, the more you'll communicate to your newlywed bride that you love her, not just her sexuality. You'd be surprised how many newlywed wives come back home from the honeymoon and tell their friends that they never had a clue before marriage about how intense and overpowering their husbands' sex drive was. Don't behave so that you could become the subject of such discussions with your wife's friends. (We advise her not to discuss such personal things with friends anyway!)

Wives, by your attitude and behavior, make it clear to your husband that he is more important to you than anything in the world. Be as free and open in your expressions of love as you can. Recognize that his desire for you is directly related to his love for you as a person. The more he knows that he's your one and only, the one on whom you want to shower all your physical and emotional affection, the more he will treat you as his queen.

Honeymoon Cystitis

Honeymoon cystitis is a bladder infection that women sometimes contract after having intercourse. It often occurs during the honeymoon when a woman becomes sexually active for the first time. Generally, most women gradually develop a resistance to such infections. However, some women have recurrent symptoms related to intercourse and may need to take prophylactic antibiotics (an antibiotic just prior to or just after each sexual encounter).

This infection can be easily treated with antibiotics, but you need to be aware of the symptoms. The urge to urinate all of the time, even when your bladder is not full, painful urination, and an increase in the frequency of urination are all signs of a bladder infection. There are some basic things you can do to decrease the risk of developing honeymoon cystitis. Be sure to drink plenty of fluids (until the urine is almost colorless). Drink cranberry juice because it reduces the bacteria associated with urinary tract infections. And empty your bladder before and immediately after intercourse. If you begin to experience any symptoms, continue to follow these suggestions and, if it is feasible, see a doctor (or call yours) to obtain antibiotics. If you have a history of frequent urinary tract infections, you may want to ask your doctor to prescribe an antibiotic at your premarital exam. That way you can begin to take the antibiotic immediately if any symptoms occur and you won't have to search for a doctor on your honeymoon.

THE WEDDING DAY AND NIGHT

It is common for the last few days leading to your wedding day and night to be very hectic. Listed below are a few suggestions which may help make this important day and night more enjoyable.

- Both the bride and groom need to get a full night's sleep prior to the wedding. This is best accomplished by setting your deadline to be done with all the planning and preparation two or three days prior to the wedding day.

- Brides (and grooms!) need to eat breakfast even if they feel they are too nervous to do so. We recommend foods that are broken down slowly and that are not greasy, for example, oatmeal, fruit, yogurt, and toast made with whole wheat.

- Consider having the reception on a different night than the wedding. If that is not possible, have the wedding late morning or early afternoon and the reception early in the evening.

- Be sure to eat and drink adequately during the day and at the reception. At the reception, have someone bring you drinks and snacks even though you are busy greeting well wishers.

- If possible, have some of the wedding pictures taken prior to the wedding day.

- Don't drive long distances the day after the wedding. You will be more tired than you think.

- Schedule airline flights in the early afternoon rather than in the morning. Better yet, leave one day after the wedding for your honeymoon.

Chapter Five

For the Husband

How to Treat Your Wife

If you treat your wife like a queen, she'll respond as if you were a king. During your courtship you treated her like a queen. You were funny, sensitive, attentive, and you did everything in your power to favorably impress her so that she would be thrilled with you. In short, you met both her emotional and romantic needs. This is likely a large part of why she became interested in and aroused by you. It is not, as most men believe, just their great looks.

Unfortunately most husbands don't continue their courtship after marriage. Yet their wives' romantic and emotional desires do continue, and they will resent it if they are taken for granted after the wedding. Don't become less sensitive. Continue to provide emotional support and nurture your relationship like you did prior to marriage. If you don't, should it be a great surprise that her sexual interest in you decreases as your emotional interest in her decreases? Continuing your emotional courtship will actually enhance and nurture your sexual relationship.

In these days of hectic schedules, in which school, work, church, family, and friends may compete for your time, married couples often don't spend enough meaningful time together. If you want a close and rewarding relationship with your wife, you must make time for her. The Church advises you to take your sweetheart on a weekly date. The date should be something that gives the two of you a chance to be together by yourselves. It should be fun for both, as you pursue your mutual interests, and should give you a time to focus on each other. This date should not be a time where you discuss problems. Problems and concerns should be left at home. There will be time enough later to discuss problems. In fact, you might find the problems disappearing if you continue your courtship after marriage.

HELPING YOUR WIFE FEEL LOVED MAKES SEX BETTER FOR YOU

For most women, the emotional aspects of the sexual relationship are more important than the actual physical acts of sex, although the two are very closely intertwined. Women value sex because it makes them feel loved as much as or more than because it is physically pleasurable. Knowing she is loved, secure, beautiful, and special to you allows your wife to become more easily sexually aroused. Without this emotional support, she may mistakenly feel like her body is being used and that you don't appreciate her as a total person. She may feel that your love for her is only physical, rather than the deeper love that you feel for her.

For many women, verbally expressing their feelings helps them feel more loving and more attracted to their husbands. However, for a woman to open up and express her feelings, she must be emotionally secure in her relationship with you. It's important for your wife to know you want and desire her.

A country-western song of some years ago comes to mind. In this song the husband tells his wife that she's "close enough to perfect for him." Truly, a man should feel this way about his wife. If, at the present time, you do not, then you have some work to do in opening your eyes to her qualities and strengths. Of course it is important that she is physically attractive to you, but even more important is that you see her internal qualities and talents such as her intelligence, understanding, and compassion, and that you understand her divine worth as a daughter of God.

If you haven't taken notice of these attributes, take some time alone and list everything that's good about your wife on a notepad. Be sincere in your thinking and avoid making any criticism whatsoever in your mind. Then share with her what you've discovered or rediscovered about her, without the slightest hint of criticism. When you truly see her as "close enough to perfect for you," both your love for her and her love for you will increase substantially. Very likely your wife's strengths and qualities equal or exceed yours!

Showing and telling her that you admire and appreciate these qualities will strengthen your relationship both emotionally and sexually. If you don't take care of her emotional needs, she'll have no desire to take care of your sexual needs; and if she tries to do so, it will likely be without her full emotional and physical involvement. If that occurs, sex won't be truly fulfilling for either of you. Until her emotional needs are met, she'll be unable to give herself completely to you.

"Honey, Why Don't You Stop and Ask for Directions?"

The reason most men refuse to stop and ask directions is they don't want to look or feel inadequate, not in charge, or weak. It may be true that many men's egos are more fragile than women's. This is a result of the way men are raised in this society. Men are brought up to believe themselves in charge, or that they should be when they've grown up. Men think they're weak if they don't have all the answers and aren't in charge and in control of everything significant to them. However, if you fail to ask about how your wife feels and how her body works and what she wants, you may never know what excites her physically and sexually.

It has been said that the secret to a happy marriage is to determine who is boss and then listen to her. This is also true for sexual intimacies. Contrary to what you may have been told, there are no road maps about your wife's particular needs and desires. She's unique in what she likes and dislikes. Further, her needs and desires change from year to year, month to month, day to day, and even hour to hour. She's the only one who can tell you what she feels and how she wants to be touched and caressed. The only way for you to know how to meet her wants and give her what she wants is to ask her for directions. Remember, what worked for you yesterday may not work today. She's her own best guide, and you must follow her lead. Even though you think you know what you are doing, her desires will change frequently and you must be receptive to her directions. To be skillful in bed, you must ask her and listen to her.

Men tend to like routines. They establish them at work and even in their recreational and leisure pursuits. Once they've found the best route to the job or to the fishing hole or to the football stadium, they want to go that way from then on. "Why change?" they ask. "Hey, it was the best way to get there yesterday and last week. Why not go the same way today?"

Women don't like routines as much as men, particularly in bed. They'd rather be creative and do it different ways. "If we don't take a different highway this time, who knows what beautiful scenery we may have missed?" It's the same when your wife expresses her love for you and the way you express yours to her. Always seek her input. Always be open to different ideas she might have. Don't try to force your old routine on her. Remember, for her, things that lead up to the "main event" are often more important than "the event" itself.

UNDERSTANDING A WOMAN

Completely understanding a woman may not be possible, but the following points may help. Men want more than anything to have an orgasm. Women want to be loved by touching, kissing, caressing, holding, and being close. If you push for what is most exciting to you, you'll rob her of her greatest pleasure, and the inevitable result will be that her love for you will decrease because you will have demonstrated to her that what you want is more important to you than what she wants. Such insensitivity is a major mistake.

You are like a microwave oven—easily turned on and quickly turned off. Your wife is much more like a conventional oven. She needs time to heat up and just as much time to cool down. Your wife needs to be touched and caressed before and after sexual intercourse. She needs more touching and caressing than you do. Most of the time, you're ready much sooner than she is. Sexual intercourse and penetration too early isn't only unpleasant for a woman, it is often painful. She may not tell you this because she doesn't want to hurt your feelings, or she thinks it's her problem when, in truth, it's yours. If this becomes a regular pattern, your wife will very likely begin to avoid any physical affection that might lead to sex. That's not because she doesn't love you; it's because sex has become unpleasant and possibly painful. If you don't take enough time to caress and touch her both before and after intercourse, it will be very hard for her to continue to believe that you truly care for her; she may believe you are only concerned for yourself. So don't follow your instincts; take the time to understand your wife.

If you do what comes naturally when it comes to making love to your wife, most of the time you'll be wrong! We've mentioned several times that your wife doesn't respond sexually the way you do, and what you want is usually not exactly what your wife wants. It's both amazing and appalling just how many young men take so long to learn this lesson. Popular music, movies, TV shows, magazines, books, and other media fail miserably in properly educating young men (and women) about romance and sex.

Dr. Lindsay Curtis, a noted LDS medical doctor, wrote: "A woman is like a beautiful orchestra. She must first be warmed up and tuned. Then delicately and slowly the various instruments must be brought into play in order for the music to be harmonious and moving. Harshly played, a beautiful and inspiring work becomes unbearable and offensive. But like the orchestra, intimate relationships must be practiced with the parties involved communicating closely together to achieve the desired results."[9]

To understand your wife's needs and wants, you must learn to use good communication skills. Admit to her that you're inexperienced and that she needs to teach you how her mind and body work. Do all that you can to communicate to her that her wishes and desires are uppermost in your mind and always will be. This should include not only her desires for affection and sex, but all her desires in life. You'll be surprised at what you learn, and you will find ways of satisfying her that you never would have dreamed of before your heart-to-heart talks. Then follow through by showing her you mean what you say.

Establishing honest and forthright communication is only the beginning. Your wife needs time to herself and time to relax. This means you may have to help relieve some of the home pressures for her. Often, the most important foreplay you can provide is to help her with the household chores or the needs of the kids so that she has the time and energy to be sexual. Then once your wife has the time and energy for making love you must still kindle her desire.

Kenny Rogers sang, "A woman loves a man with a slow hand." This is one of the most important things you can learn about your wife. While simply the thought of a sexual encounter with your wife can be physically arousing to you, for her, cuddling, touching, and stroking are often more important to her than the actual act of intercourse.

While a man needs about two to three minutes of stimulation to achieve an orgasm or climax, a woman requires fifteen to twenty minutes of stimulation to achieve an orgasm. It is very important that you not communicate either verbally or nonverbally that you do not wish to touch or stroke her clitoris, or that you are tired of it, or that you are comparing how slow she is in coming as compared to you. This is a major mistake. Make sure that you communicate effectively that your major desire is that she be satisfied with your lovemaking. Make it your goal to have her satisfied with how you make love with her. This is why Dr. Helen Kaplan, a noted authority and sex therapist, has pointed out that the only true aphrodisiac is love.[10] That means, when your wife is convinced by your verbal and nonverbal behavior that you truly love her, and that her pleasure is uppermost in your mind, she will become totally aroused by you and want you to be fulfilled too.

Mutually satisfying intercourse occurs when both of you have had your desires fulfilled. For you, orgasm is almost always enough. Depending on your wife's desire, she can and should experience orgasm. However, most women say they don't require an orgasm every time to be satisfied. Sometimes loving, physical contact is all your wife will want or need; she might just forego reaching orgasm. But the loving contact is always essential in order for her to be pleased. Masters and Johnson found that "a woman is not necessarily lacking in sexual responsiveness when she does not experience an orgasm. Therefore, the achievement of orgasmic response should not be considered the end all of sexual gratification for the responding female. But, if she rarely achieves an orgasm she may become sexually frustrated and will become less interested in sex. In fact, for a wife, always being sexually unfulfilled can be emotionally traumatic."[11] So let your wife decide whether she wants an orgasm. Don't make the decision for her by hastening yours.

After experiencing mutually rewarding physical contact, you will feel closer to her than at any other time. Take time to hold and enjoy being with her. Recognize that your wife wants and needs to be held after intercourse. This is the best time to say, "I love you. I love what you do for me. You're everything to me. You make me feel so good. I love you." This is not the time to roll over and go to sleep. This is the time that you truly show your love for her, not during intercourse. If you handle this time well, it will help pave the way for your next encounter. Your wife will remember your tenderness and love and be more inclined to fulfill your needs. If, however, you treat this time unwisely (by just turning over and going to sleep) she will be unfulfilled and question your love and caring. Thus she will be less inclined to participate in sex the next time.

Becoming a Great Lover—Before the Bedroom

To become a great lover, what you do outside the bedroom is just as important as what you do inside. Ask and answer these two questions: "What can I do to please my wife most?" and "How does she feel about what I do?" If you can provide her with the physical pleasure and emotional security that she desires, your physical pleasure will be greatly increased. If you want to be sexually satisfied, make sure to first satisfy your wife. When a woman discusses her most memorable sexual experiences, she discusses how her partner touched her and made her feel important and loved. When men talk about their most memorable sexual experiences, they talk about how they were able to excite and physically satisfy their partner. In other words, both the husband and the wife will find the greatest sexual satisfaction in the same thing; that is, when she has had a great sexual experience. The more emotionally connected you are to your wife, the more her pleasure becomes yours.

The following are important tips on becoming a good lover:

- Be affectionate in nondemanding ways. Touch your wife lovingly at times when you don't necessarily expect more to follow so that a touch can be an expression of love in her mind and not just a request for intercourse.

- Protect her privacy. Never discuss your sexual intimacies with anyone, including your best friends, parents, relatives, or associates. To violate this trust will put an instant distance between you and your wife. Once trust has been violated, it takes at least twice as long to rebuild it as it did to build in the first place.

- Learn as much as you can about your wife—not just in the area of affection and sex, but in every possible way. Make her truly the most important person and thing in your life. Find out all her likes and dislikes, and try your best to fulfill as many of her likes as you can (not just sexually, but in every other way too). Talk to her alone and often. Find out what makes her tick. Try to understand her reasoning about the subjects that interest her. Contribute your part, especially when she asks you for your thoughts and feelings.

- Demonstrate self-control in everything you do. We already know that as a man, you want to feel that you are in control of your life. You don't want to be controlled by anyone else, so why would you let circumstances control your reactions? This applies to your whole life. For example, don't lose control and swear at another driver on the highway; don't upbraid a referee for a bad call on the basketball court; don't yell at your wife—ever. Show restraint. Show your wife that you're in control of yourself by not hurrying her during lovemaking.

- Focus your lovemaking on her satisfaction. Don't start out thinking you have a right to sexual satisfaction just because she's your wife and you've been married in the temple. If she gets the idea that your pushiness is an integral part of you and that you'll take that impatience with you into the life hereafter, don't be surprised if she doesn't want to be part of that kind of relationship. The true leader, whether in regard to his family, church, business, government, or even sex will put the interests and desires of others before his own. In our professional experience we find that a significant number of men have trouble with this principle; don't be one of them.

- Don't ever forget what arouses your wife. Remember what she has told you about herself and her desires. Be aware of what she wants and be aware that this will change frequently.

- Avoid talking about your wife behind her back. If there are things you wish she'd do differently, or ways you would like her to be (including physical attributes such as weight and appearance) don't ever discuss these issues with anyone but your wife. It's no one else's business. If friends or associates talk about their wives behind their backs, or if some tell jokes or in other ways demean their wives, refuse to engage in such destructive actions.

- Use endearing, loving language with your wife and avoid using language she finds offensive, even if you think it will turn her on. If she doesn't enjoy it, you're foolish to insist on using it. Some misguided men think that having their wives watch X- or R-rated movies is a good way to get them aroused. Don't do it. General Authorities have warned against such movies and entertainment. If it's wrong to engage in illicit sexual activities, surely it's wrong to watch them performed before a camera. Most important, your wife wants to be your most desirable sexual object. When you engage in the viewing of pornographic material you are telling her that she is not enough to satisfy your sexual needs. This is very damaging to a relationship. It is perverse and wrong.

- Love her as a person and don't ever criticize. Criticizing your wife lessens her love for you and lessens her desire to be intimate. And being critical in lovemaking is an invitation for disaster. Research shows that criticism always puts distance between the person being criticized and the person doing the criticizing. It doesn't take education, knowledge, or brains to criticize, and often those who engage in criticizing leave their education, knowledge, and common sense behind when they begin to criticize. Don't let this happen in your marriage, which is the most significant and important relationship you will ever have.

- Be aware of offensive body odors. A woman's sexual arousal can be a fragile thing, and an offensive odor can undo hours of flirting, courtship, and foreplay. Before making love, empty your bladder, shave, shower, and put on her favorite cologne. Your wife is the one person who you should want to impress the most. Remember your good grooming habits when you were courting? Your wife doesn't want to make love to a scratchy, smelly bear. That's not sexy, even if the commercials you see on TV say so. You need to arouse all of her senses, including her sense of smell. Remember, the sense of smell is far more important in regards to sexual arousal for women than for men. If a smell would turn you off, it will be more so for your wife. Men who practice good body hygiene prior to going to bed will find it time well spent.

Becoming a Great Lover—In the Bedroom

Generally speaking, men are more visual, women are more verbal. Telling your wife what you like about her and how she makes you feel will frequently arouse her as much as your physical touch or anything you do. Below are some examples of ways to express how your wife makes you feel. Some women love and need to hear these things during actual lovemaking; for others it is more important to hear them "before the bedroom."

I love you.

I love sharing my life with you.

You sure turn me on.

I love to touch your . . . (skin, hair, lips, etc.).

Your . . . (legs, lips, eyes, etc.) turn me on.

I love holding you.

You feel so good to me.

You're so delicious.

I am all yours.

I love making love to you.

All my love is yours.

I am only for you.

I want you forever.

You're beautiful (gorgeous, ravishing, etc.).

Above all, say what you sincerely feel in words your wife will know are your own. Notice that you should make references to her physical attributes last. Most women want to be loved for who they are, not just for their physical beauty. While it is important to tell your wife she's beautiful, just be sure to say these other things as well. This communicates to her more effectively that you truly love her as a person.

Avoid being mechanical in the way you approach making love. Often men have a tendency to find one way that works for them and then repeat it over and over. Most men feel that "If it ain't broke don't fix it." But sexual intimacy is sort of like watching sports. If you know the final score, it isn't as much fun to watch. It's the anticipation of what's going to happen next that makes both sports and sex exciting. Treat each sexual experience a little differently. Touch and stroke a new direction. Go from one area to another in a different order. Try various positions. Try different locations. Be spontaneous and varied in your sexual experience and activities.

Begin your sexual relationship with your wife long before taking your clothes off. Touch her in areas that she enjoys and that are away from sexually sensitive areas. Massage her back, neck, and feet. Make caressing and loving motions in the direction of her erogenous areas, but don't actually touch them. Let her feel your need by touching your sensitive areas to hers without even the hint of penetration. Start to remove her clothes, then stop, and then start again. Let her anticipate your movements, but continue to be slow to touch her erogenous areas. Let her love and desire for you grow slowly. Once clothes have been removed for both of you, continue touching and caressing her in areas that are away from her erogenous zones. Then, very slowly move toward, and then away from these sensitive areas. It's best to gradually lead to the places where she wants to be touched. Let her guide you when and to where she wants to be touched and caressed. This allows her to relax and let go of her inhibitions. Practice going slowly. Remember, it takes up to ten times longer for your wife to achieve orgasm than for you.

As she begins to become aroused, gently and briefly touch her nipples or clitoris. Ask her to guide you to the appropriate areas. Never rush. A touch that's too hard or too long may actually produce pain and a loss of sexual interest. Remember, for your wife to become aroused, the anticipation of your touch or act is as important as is the touch itself. As your wife becomes more aroused you can spend more time touching and caressing her erogenous areas.

When she becomes aroused, the glands around the opening of her vagina secrete a lubricating fluid that seeps though the vaginal mucosa membrane resulting in the feeling of her being wet. However, vaginal and vulva lubrication doesn't always mean she's ready for penetration. Before penetration occurs, additional stimulation by stroking or touching her clitoris is often needed to bring her closer to orgasm.

If she would like, help your wife experience a climax before penetration. If she has one or more climaxes prior to penetration, her sexual excitement will be at a peak, and she will be more able to provide what you want and need. When penetration is delayed until after orgasm, she will be very wet and penetration will be easy and pleasurable for both of you. She may want to move in complementary fashion as you make your thrusts into her. Her excitement and arousal will excite and arouse you even more than you were before. Usually within a few seconds, you will experience your orgasm too. Sometimes, when you feel yourself about to come, you will want to delay your climax and stop moving. This is fine. If you are able to calm a little, until the sensation of coming subsides, then you can begin again. This will heighten both your and your wife's excitement even more.

Making love with your wife is something that is and should be ever changing. You have heard the saying that practice makes perfect. We're sure that perfection is not ever achieved in this life, particularly when it involves a husband and a wife's sexual relationship. But as you work (which really isn't work) to fulfill each other's needs and desires, focusing first on your wife's needs, your sexual and affectional relationship will become more and more enjoyable and your love for each other will increase. You'll find that you can together face the world and its trials and struggles more effectively and with a better attitude. Best of all, you will have created something between yourselves that is unique and wonderful. This strong physical relationship will draw you more closely together and unite you as a couple.

Chapter Six

For the Wife

Understanding Your Husband

Many women underestimate the importance of sex for men. The most powerful way a women's love can touch a man's soul is through sex. In most cases, it's sex, not the stomach, which proves to be the most direct way to a man's heart. When a man is satisfied sexually, his ability to feel joy, love, closeness, compassion, caring, and peace is tremendously increased. In a normal and healthy marital relationship, your husband needs to feel free to initiate sex (as do you).

Since men are so direct in their desire for sexual gratification, often women tend to judge them too harshly. Sometimes they interpret men's desire for sex as being frivolous and self-centered. However, in truth, that's usually not so. Though a man's sex drive is strong at a young age and persists for most of his life, sex is, for him, the most effective way he can show his wife that he loves her. For a husband, the sex act is something that he feels is the best way of showing his wife that he loves her.

You also must understand the physical and physiologic importance of sex for men. While women can have a very strong desire and need for sex, this need is usually more emotional than physical. For men the physical need for sex is much stronger. Extended periods of time without intercourse may lead to physical discomfort from unreleased semen. Even if he doesn't feel physical discomfort, if a man's sexual needs aren't being met he may become irritable or more easily frustrated or may just feel things aren't going well in his life. However, if a man is happy in his sexual relationship, all other areas of his life and all their problems seem easier to handle.

Granted, your husband has much to learn when it comes to lovemaking and effectively showing you his love. He has to learn to be caring, compassionate, patient, kind, gentle, and loving. For him, the most direct route seems like it would be the best. "Surely," he thinks, "if I can hardly keep from attacking her and taking what I want, that will prove to her how much I truly love her." A young husband may mistakenly think that if he's forceful in expressing his sexual arousal to the wife he loves, she can't fail to see how much he loves her. He has much to learn about himself and especially about his wife. So, be patient. It will take time for your husband to learn about you, lovemaking, and marriage.

Generally you must be emotionally close to your husband before you begin to feel physically aroused. Your husband, on the other hand, is most open to accept love and emotional support during sexual arousal. For your husband, sexual arousal helps him to open his heart to your love. You may have a difficult time understanding this aspect of your husband. It's probably very strange to you that sex can be on his mind as soon as he walks in the door after having been at work all day. You may think, "If he really loves me, why does he go after sex so soon? How come he can't see that I need some closeness first, that I need to have some peace of mind and heart? Why doesn't he realize that problems with money, kids, work, the house, or other things need to be resolved, or at least discussed, before I can feel loving and sexual?"

If he answered these questions for you, he'd probably say something like: "When we have sex, sweetheart, I feel like I can take on the world all by myself. I just know that any problems we have will almost disappear and that I'll be able to handle everything just fine. If we have sex, I'll know you really love me, and then I can focus all my energy on getting things done that need doing. I promise, everything is going to be all right. Don't you know, I love you more than anyone could ever love anyone else? Of course I want to have sex with you. It's the best way I know to show you how much I love you."

Just thinking of his love for you makes him want to have sex, whereas, for you, thinking about your love for him makes you want to sit close together, look into his eyes, talk about important things in your relationship, set some goals, or just hold him and be close—but not necessarily anything sexual—at least, not right away.

Another frequent problem is that, secretly, a wife may think that if her husband really loved her, he'd instinctively know what she wants and doesn't want. You may tend to think that if he's so in love with you, he'll know what turns you on. He seemed to know it before you were married. He was always doing sweet, nice, loving things for you. Now he seems to want to jump in bed before doing anything sweet or nice at all.

The truth is, your husband does not instinctively know what you want most of the time. But the fact that he can't read your mind does not mean he doesn't love you. However, if you just sit and wait for him to learn how to be caring and make love effectively, you will be waiting for a long time. You need to teach him. He truly doesn't know what's meaningful and important to you. The fact is, when he was growing up, he hardly paid any attention at all to what his mother wanted or needed, and certainly he had no clue about his big sister. It simply wasn't important to him.

However, you are important to him. Now he just needs to learn what makes you feel good in your marriage relationship, and he needs you to tell him those things. He needs you to be direct with him about what feels good both emotionally and physically. For example, you might tell him, "You know what would really get me in the mood right now? A nice foot massage." Or, "I could really use some time to just talk with you right now. Do you mind turning off the TV for a while?" The fact that you have to ask him first in no way should decrease the value or meaning of the things he does for you. Also, you should make sure that you thank him and let him know how great it makes you feel when he does nice things for you without being asked. Noticing his efforts will make you both feel better about each other and will make him more likely to do similar things in the future.

Your husband also needs to learn from you when he is being insensitive and why it's insensitive. Don't tell him in an attacking way, of course, but let him know that his dirty clothes lying on the floor makes it hard for you to feel love for him. You need to say that leaving his whiskers in the sink after he shaves is a real turnoff. There are many similar types of things he needs to learn. These things are different for every woman, and it really isn't fair for a woman to expect her husband to somehow know these things without being told.

Many women do not understand that it is necessary for them to instruct their husbands in the area of sexuality. Your greatest sexual skill will be your ability to help your husband be successful in fulfilling your sexual needs. The only part of sex that your husband enjoys more than orgasm itself is the satisfied feeling he gains from knowing that he has satisfied you and that you find him sexually exciting. There's no greater truth about lovemaking for a man than that. When you're aroused, you're actually giving your husband what he needs and desires most. For this reason, you are not being selfish when you tell your husband what to do or what feels good to you. You should not be afraid to ask him to help you enjoy sex. He will likely get just as much pleasure as you do from your sexual satisfaction.

If your husband feels he has failed in satisfying you sexually, his ego will be deflated and he may begin to tell himself that there's something wrong with him or you. Remember, his ego is much more fragile than yours because of the way society teaches young males. Yet, if he does not understand what your sexual needs are, he won't understand why he hasn't been able to satisfy you sexually. He might become frustrated and even angry.

In subtle ways, your husband "reads" you and you "read" him. Often your reading of each other is absolutely wrong, and the assumptions you both make can be destructive. Resolve to be open and honest about what you need and want. He'll be happy to hear it! He's not going to tell you to be quiet about what you want him to do when it comes to sex. If you don't let him know what you want and like, your sexual needs won't be satisfied and your husband's sexual satisfaction will also be less than what either of you want it to be.

Before you can teach your husband what you enjoy, you may need to learn what arouses you. In order for you to be sexually stimulated and gain your greatest sexual satisfaction, you must understand that you require more time than your partner; your clitoris is the center of your sexual experience; and time, exploration, experience, and practice are required for you to learn how to become orgasmic.

This cannot be achieved if you and your partner are overly inhibited in conversations about sex and your sexual experiences together.

Remember he is now your husband. All those things they told you in church when you were dating that you shouldn't do or talk about are no longer off limits. You don't have to be uncomfortable talking with your husband about sex anymore. Even if it feels uncomfortable at first, the more you talk about sex with your husband, the easier (and more fun) it will get.

Getting in the Mood

Having a close, loving, and fulfilling sexual relationship with your husband is one of the most important things you can have in your healthy marriage relationship. Men and women exist that they might have joy (2 Ne. 2:25). Heavenly Father wants you to have a healthy and happy sexual relationship with your husband. He didn't make a mistake by giving you and your husband these feelings and urges. Therefore, it's right for you to pray and ask for a wonderful sexual experience. At first this may sound strange to you, but wives and husbands often pray about less important areas of their relationship. You may find that you feel closer emotionally to your husband right after you've prayed together than at any other time. Therefore, it's at this time that you may be the most sexually attracted to him. Don't be afraid to show him those feelings. If you follow this advice, you may find him wanting to pray with you more often.

In addition to praying alone and together, doing anything that helps you feel warm, sensual, and attractive will increase your desire for sexual stimulation. For example, take a long and relaxing bath prior to engaging in sexual relations. Wear clothes that make you feel attractive or sexy, put on your favorite perfume, or ask for a massage from your husband.

Having a positive mental attitude toward sexual relations is also very important. It may take time. That's okay, but take the time to develop it. Remember, your two most sensitive sex organs are your clitoris and your mind. You will not be satisfied sexually if you don't have a positive attitude about sex.

However, you should not feel abnormal or inadequate if your sexual drive does not seem as strong as your husband's. In fact, many sexually healthy women rarely or never feel a strong desire for sex before it begins. They start a sexual experience because of a desire for closeness or to express love to their husband, and then as they become aroused they feel more sexual desire. Recent research by Dr. Rosemary Basson and others indicates that this may be a more common pattern for women than the traditional model of Masters and Johnson (see chapter 3) where first desire leads to arousal which then leads to sexual excitement and climax. For many women, arousal comes before desire.[12]

Another way of explaining this idea is that sometimes sex is like waterskiing. When the water is cold and you are warm and dry in the boat, it's hard to be the first one to volunteer to go out on waterskis. But after that first plunge into the water, when you're up and flying across the water on skis, you're having a great time and don't want to stop. Sometimes in sex, as in waterskiing, you just have to jump in, even if you don't feel like it at first. You'll almost always be glad you did.

LIGHT HIS FIRE

Men tend to be visual and easily stimulated by sight. Partly because of this fact, LDS young women are taught to dress and think modestly and to keep their bodies covered to a standard above that observed by much of the rest of the world. This is still very appropriate in public. But in private, after the wedding, you need to lay aside your inhibitions and overcome your sense of modesty if you desire to give your deepest love to your husband. As long as you both feel comfortable and there is no coercion, what occurs in the bedroom is between you and your husband. Within the bonds of marriage pleasurable touches and caresses can and should be given and received freely without feelings of guilt.

Enjoy the fact that you are beautiful to your husband. Since men are visually oriented your husband will enjoy seeing your unclothed body. Don't worry that your body isn't exactly what you'd like it to be. Nobody is perfect. Don't be concerned with what you perceive as your physical imperfections. Unless you point them out, he probably won't notice what you consider to be flaws, especially when he is aroused.

Since men are stimulated by sight, it's important to try to look your best for him. If you wouldn't go out in public in baggy sweats, no makeup, and messy hair, why would you want your husband to see you that way on a regular basis? Isn't he at least as important as your girlfriends or the strangers at the grocery store? Look in the mirror like you did before going out with him when you were dating. Observe good daily feminine hygiene. You might even dress in something sexy. This will tell him that you are interested in him and want to please him. Feeling that he turns you on is extremely important to your husband's ego.

Even though you dress modestly in public, realize that in the privacy of your bedroom, revealing clothing can often be more sexy and seductive than being completely naked. Sheer night clothes will enhance your body's attractiveness the way a soft screen improves the effect of a photograph. Sometimes it's best to leave something to his imagination; but sometimes it's not. You decide.

Some therapists suggest that you wear nightclothes based on your mood. For example, red could be for when you're feeling adventurous; blue might be for when you want him to take time and be seductive. Consider wearing black when you want to be the aggressor.

Don't be afraid to take the lead and be assertive. Nothing feeds your husband's ego more than the feeling that his wife wants and needs him in a sexual way. However, don't always be the initiator. If he feels pressured to perform all of the time, this can make it more difficult for him to perform even at other times when he's taking the initiative.

Regardless of who initiates it, actively participate in making love to your husband. While men may not require as much caressing and touching as women do to become aroused, they certainly enjoy it. Touching and stimulating his erogenous zones will increase his pleasure and help show your love for him. Let him tell you how and where to touch. Wives need instruction from their husbands just as husbands do from their wives in order to become better lovers.

A woman's sexual responsiveness is a powerful way for a man to feel he is loved. His feelings of love for his wife are then rekindled. When a wife longs for sex, she's open and trusting; she makes her husband feel accepted, appreciated, and loved. Go out of your way to let your husband know that he is a good lover and that you enjoy his advances and your sexual relationship with him.

Additional Helpful Suggestions

- You should never fake an orgasm (climax). It is understandable that you want your husband to feel he's a successful lover. But as in all other situations in your marriage, honesty is vital in the bedroom. Further, faking orgasms may make it harder to have them in the future. It's normal and common for women, especially early on in your sexual relationship, to be unable to achieve an orgasm at times. If, at times, you are able to feel fulfilled and satisfied with your sexual experience without having an orgasm, tell him so. When the two of you communicate effectively, he will understand that you can be satisfied with him sexually without having to climax every time, and he will then feel comfortable if you do not want or are unable to climax every time. If at other times you are having difficulty reaching orgasm but want or need to, you should also tell him, so he can continue to help you achieve climax and in the process learn things that will help make it easier the next time. Women who are never, or almost never, given the opportunity to climax will begin to avoid sex as well as those situations that may lead to sex, which isn't good for either of you.

- During intercourse is the optimal time to practice Kegel exercises (see chapter 4). Women who perform this strengthening exercise of the pelvic muscles regularly find that their sexual satisfaction measurably improves.

- Sometimes, in order to make intercourse more comfortable for both the wife and husband, it is helpful to use an additional lubricating substance. The section "Lubrication" in the next chapter discusses this in greater detail.

Chapter Seven

Some Important Details

An attitude of openness and frankness is essential in your marriage. It's absolutely imperative that the two of you communicate openly. If your sex education in school or at home was less than adequate, seek information about human anatomy and physiology in the library or on appropriate internet sites. Reviewing or learning this information together will help open up discussions and set a basis for common knowledge and understanding. While volumes have been written regarding sexual positions and technique, it all comes down to what works specifically for you as a couple. Don't be afraid to explore and try new things.

As a wife, you can show your love by being openly responsive to your husband's physical advances. Nothing will show him that you love him more than your willingness and desire to take him into yourself. As a husband, remember that for your wife, being loved in nonsexual ways is often more important than actually participating in sexual relations. Tell her often and in many ways that she's loved. It's a husband's emotional responsiveness and a wife's physical responsiveness that provide the ingredients needed to create a physically passionate marriage.

Romance

Before her sexual desire can be aroused, your wife needs to be romanced. Yet many men don't understand what romance means to a woman. Romance can be summarized by one concept: a good lover shows his wife both in words and by what he does that she is the most important thing in his life. When you perform spontaneous acts of love for your wife, particularly when the occasion doesn't require it (birthdays and anniversaries don't count), you're romancing your wife. This will ignite the flames of passion faster and more surely than anything else you can do.

Romancing your wife means making her feel she's more important than your job, friends, or family. This means finding time for her that is free from interruptions from outside sources. Taking a weekend or even one night away from the kids, job, and the pager will go a long way to provide the romance she is craving. (When you decide to do this, it is double the points if you are the one who arranges for a babysitter, not your wife.) It also means spending time involved in activities that she wants to do, even if you clearly dislike them. Shopping, strolling, or spending an evening just talking can do wonders for your romantic relationship. (Discussing problems absolutely doesn't fit into this category.) Sometimes awakening her desires can be as simple as bringing home flowers, cleaning up the kitchen, changing messy diapers, putting a load of clothes in the washer, straightening the living room, and, definitely, cleaning up after yourself.

Providing privacy is something else you should consider in setting the stage for a sexual encounter. Many people, especially women, find it much easier to relax and enjoy sex if they know the doors are locked, the blinds are closed, and there is no chance of outside interruption or observation. You may even want to take the phone off the hook. While some people enjoy the danger factor that comes with less-than-guaranteed privacy, everyone is different and you should respect your spouse's wishes with regard to privacy issues.

FOREPLAY

Foreplay can be magic. Yet, it's probably the most often neglected part of sexual relations. Foreplay, sexual play before actual intercourse, starts before you go to bed. It may begin with simple flirting, something most couples get plenty of practice at during their courtship. It may be as simple as a touch, a wink, or intimate whispers minutes to hours before entering your bedroom. Sometimes it may be more elaborate in the form of a fantasy or game. Once you enter the bedroom (or whatever room), foreplay may involve touching, undressing, and kissing. Caresses should usually be gentle, light, fleeting, and teasing in nature. The amount of time spent in foreplay is as important as technique. While every woman is different in the amount of time required, as a general rule it will require fifteen to twenty minutes for her to become fully aroused.

Lubrication

When aroused, women secrete a fluid in and around the vagina that helps lubricate the area prior to penetration. Women in good health and whose bodies function properly, produce sufficient lubrication for intercourse when they are satisfactorily aroused. Sufficient lubrication takes longer for some women than for others. When this is the case, it merely means that foreplay should be extended, with husbands exercising greater patience and understanding. Sometimes, however, using a lubricant is helpful or even necessary. A few women don't ever secrete enough fluid and may require additional lubrication in order to prevent pain. This becomes more common as women approach menopause. Lubricants are often helpful after childbirth, especially if you are breast-feeding. And sometimes doctors advise the use of an additional lubricating substance. This is particularly true for first intercourse experiences.

K-Y Jelly has been the lubricant most frequently used and recommended, but K-Y Jelly becomes sticky with use and can actually cause irritation. Astroglide is another widely available lubricant with a more natural feel. Some physicians recommend baby oil, which not only lubricates, but will also coat the vagina and opening of the urethra, decreasing the risk of urinary tract and vaginal infections. It also has a more natural feel than K-Y Jelly. (If you are using condoms as a form of birth control, be careful. Oil breaks down the rubber and may compromise the condom's effectiveness.) Viscous lidocaine, which requires a doctor's prescription, is similar to K-Y Jelly except that it has numbing properties. For women who are very tender on the outside, it can provide welcome relief. Small tears and abrasions that may be present will be numbed by viscous lidocaine and it can significantly reduce the pain associated with these small lesions. For men who have problems with premature ejaculation, it may help by slightly desensitizing the glans and shaft of the penis, allowing for longer stimulation before climax.

We want to reiterate that additional lubrication is usually not necessary. Except in those cases where a woman does not produce sufficient natural lubrication from her own body, there can be some detrimental side effects from the frequent use of lubricants. The most serious of these side effects is a tendency to become lazy in love-making. Sufficient time must be spent in foreplay and proper arousal. The most satisfying sexual experiences take time. Indeed many women complain about the "wham-bam, thank-you-ma'am" tendencies of men. We agree. The most damaging thing to mutually satisfying sexual relations is the impatience many men demonstrate to their wives when they want an orgasm. If proper attention to foreplay and arousal is taken, in which a husband clearly demonstrates his sincere and caring love for his wife and places her pleasure before his own, it will rarely be necessary to use a lubricant.

MEN AND SELF-RESTRAINT

One of the most frequent complaints that women have regarding men is that they're like jackrabbits; they get off to a quick start and are finished before their partners have even warmed up. The best male lover understands the need to take time and provide proper stimulation. He knows if he restrains himself, his wife is more relaxed and able to enjoy sex. The more she knows he can control his sexual response and be patient, the more she can fully relax and let go, giving herself completely to him. He also knows that his wife might not be ready for him to enter her as soon as her vulva and vagina become wet. She still may need additional stimulation to bring her closer to orgasm prior to his entry. And finally, the best male lover learns how to remain in control of himself until his wife has been satisfied.

There are a few ways a man can practice control and self-restraint. After entering his wife, a husband should remain motionless until he has gained control of his sexual response. During this time she can perform Kegel exercises. This will allow her to continue to be stimulated with less risk of his climaxing prematurely.

If a woman hasn't climaxed prior to penetration and she isn't close enough to it, her husband may need to withdraw so that he dosen't ejaculate before she's ready. This can be likened to paddling a canoe down the river toward a waterfall. You can make the journey just once, or you can extend the ride by paddling to shore, getting out of the water, and walking back upstream to start again. Similarly, if the husband feels he's about to climax before his wife is ready, he can withdraw, regain control, and then he can enter his wife again. It is important when he withdraws that he continue to stimulate his wife manually so she'll be closer to climaxing when he enters her again. If, however, he climaxes before she's satisfied, it's important for him to continue to stimulate her until she's satisfied, either manually or while inside.

Remember, it doesn't matter how long a man lasts if he has first satisfied his wife. The actual act of intercourse doesn't need to be long if proper attention has been paid to proper preparation and foreplay. Intercourse (penetration) that lasts longer than about fifteen minutes can cause significant soreness for a woman's sensitive genital area.

The Physiology of an Orgasm

For both men and women, orgasm consists of a series of rapid spasmodic contractions in and around the genital organs along with an overwhelming feeling of ecstasy. It involves the entire body with increases in heart rate, blood pressure, and respiration. The explosive discharge of neuromuscular tensions at the peak of the sexual response is followed by a euphoric relaxed state of mind and body.

While being able to climax always occurs for men if sufficiently stimulated, it isn't automatic for women. Less than one-half of American women regularly achieve orgasm. In fact, some 90 percent of brides do not have orgasm during intercourse on the first attempt. Between 10 to 20 percent of married women have never achieved orgasm. We don't say this pessimistically. We only mean to point out that orgasm for women is more difficult to attain than it is for men. This emphasizes the importance of the husband's patience, tenderness, and understanding toward his wife. When the husband focuses his attention on his wife's pleasure rather than on his own, the sexual experience for both is enhanced.

For a woman, the key to orgasmic sucess is the clitoris. Every orgasm that occurs in a woman is clitoral. Women are unable to climax without direct or indirect stimulation of the clitoris. The secret is taking time during foreplay to stimulate the clitoris long enough and in such a way that she is close to orgasm prior to penetration. During intercourse, if she dosen't feel she's getting enough stimulation, she or her partner can increase clitoral stimulation either manually or with his penis.

One of the best descriptions of a female orgasm that has been written is by Dr. Marie Robinson. She wrote:

> Orgasm is the physiological response [that] brings sexual intercourse to its natural and beautiful termination. . . . In the moment just preceding orgasm, muscular tension suddenly rises to the point where, if the sexual instinct were not in operation, it would become physically unendurable. . . .
>
> At the moment of greatest muscular tension, all sensations seem to take one further rise upward. The woman tenses beyond the point where, it seems, it would be possible to maintain such tension for a moment longer. And indeed it is not possible, and now her whole body suddenly plunges into a series of muscular spasms. These spasms take place within the vagina itself, shaking the body with waves of pleasure. They are felt simultaneously throughout the body; in the torso, face, arms and legs—down to the very soles of the feet. . . .
>
> If a woman is satisfied by her orgasmic experience she will discharge the neurological and muscular tension developed in the sexual buildup. When satisfaction has been achieved, her strenuous movements cease and within a short period blood pressure, pulse, glandular secretion, muscular tension, and all the other gross physical changes [that] characterized sexual excitement, return to normal, or even to subnormal, limits. [13]

As you can see from this description, orgasm is a tremendous experience. There is no physiological or psychological experience that parallels its sweeping intensity or its excruciating pleasure. It is unique.

Women, especially newlyweds, sometimes are not sure if what they are experiencing is orgasm or not. This can be partially because women report more variation in the quality and intensity of their orgasms than men do. For men, orgasm is more of an all-or-nothing thing. For women, not all orgasms are created equal. If Dr. Robinson's description generally describes best what you are experiencing, but without all the earth-shaking intensity, you may still be experiencing orgasm. The key elements are the buildup of physical and emotional tension and the pleasurable release of that tension.

Learning to Be Orgasmic

When a woman is learning to have orgasms, her husband should provide direct manual stimulation to the clitoris and surrounding area until she is able to climax. She should direct him as to what method or intensity of stimulation brings her closer to orgasm. This will allow him to learn what works for her as well as what does not.

It is important for a woman to be able to "let go" and mentally relax enough to allow pleasure and muscular tension to build enough to reach orgasm. Too much concentrating on the goal of orgasm or self-monitoring can lead to anxiety and negative thoughts that make it more difficult to reach orgasm. In other words, don't think about it too much, and don't worry excessively if it takes a while (even weeks to months) to achieve orgasm. This is fairly common, and the important thing is making intercourse a pleasurable, not pressure-filled, experience for both of you. (If you still have not achieved orgasm after a few months you may consider seeking help from a counselor, sex therapist, self-help book, or a doctor.)

After a woman has learned how to have an orgasm from direct stimulation, her husband can stimulate her until she is close to orgasm and then enter her just prior to her climaxing. This will help her learn to climax while having intercourse. Once she regularly experiences orgasm with intercourse, couples can work on climaxing together if they wish. This requires restraint on the husband's part in conjunction with adequate romancing and foreplay prior to penetration.

Climaxing together is not always the ultimate sexual experience. Both husband and wife will often experience greater sexual satisfaction if she climaxes first. She's then able to relax and concentrate on his pleasure as well.

Must She Always Climax?

As we mentioned in chapters 5 and 6, many women do not always need to have an orgasm to be sexually fulfilled, or may not always want to have one. Women have a greater ability than men to feel fulfilled and satisfied during times of physical intimacy without climaxing. In addition, the emotional pressure of having to climax (orgasm) might actually interfere with a woman's ability to have an orgasm even though her body is ready.

Men have a difficult time understanding that, because every time they're excited, they think they must climax in order to release their sexual tension, satisfy themselves, and satisfy their wife. It can be a great relief when a man discovers that his wife may be sexually fulfilled without climaxing. On the occasions when her body is not ready to climax, she should communicate this lovingly to her husband so he doesn't feel he has failed her. This releases him to achieve an orgasm (ejaculate) without guilt. It is imperative that at those times, he then fulfills her need to be held and cuddled.

However, the fact that a wife can sometimes be sexually satisfied without reaching orgasm should *never* become an excuse for a husband to become lazy when it comes to making love. It can be a short step from there for him to begin to believe that his sexual desires can be fulfilled without taking any concern for hers. If a husband begins to believe that his wife's orgasm is not necessary, when it's taking her longer to reach orgasm than he wants, he'll begin to ask her if it's really necessary. Of course, he'll always think his orgasm is necessary! This attitude can very quickly create a dysfunctional sexual relationship between a husband and wife. So never let your sexual satisfaction become more important than her satisfaction.

Different Positions

Couples shouldn't hesitate to experiment with different positions and different types of caresses during lovemaking. This is the only way they can determine what's best for them. However, intimacy between husband and wife should never involve coercion or mistreatment in any way. That which is mutually agreeable and pleasurable, and contributes to the mutual satisfaction and enjoyment of the act is the governing factor.

Different positions can increase a couple's mutual enjoyment in lovemaking. Couples can find many ways to express their physical love and affection sexually, keeping in mind the importance of remaining sensitive to each other's needs and beliefs without offending the Spirit.

Chapter Eight

Some Potential Frustrations

As we work with couples having difficulty in their sexual relationships, we find several factors that repeatedly arise as sources of frustration and misunderstanding. You can avoid some of these if you are aware of them, and you can minimize the effects of others through good communication and hard work. Negotiating these potential pitfalls will help you have a better sexual relationship and a better marriage.

Media Focus on Marital Problems vs Marital Strengths

For many years media has focused on the problems that marriage can create, paid undo attention to high divorce rates, and refused to acknowledge the benefits of marriage. We realize that it is human nature to focus on problems rather than strengths, to see the bad rather than the good. However, in just the past couple of years we have noticed that the media has shifted focus, and some attention is now given to the benefits marriage provides for individuals and society.

Certainly the sheer number of Americans getting married should shed a positive light on marriage. First, over 90 percent of Americans marry. Second, 65–70 percent of those who marry can expect to be married to that person until one spouse dies. For highly committed marital partners, such as those choosing temple marriages, the temporal marriage rate is much higher. Third, of those in America who divorce, 75–80 percent will remarry within two or three years.[14]

We must conclude that most people want to be married. But the high percentages are not as important as why people choose to marry. New evidence is coming from many sources that points to positive physical and mental health for married persons when compared to those not married.[15]

Our message here is for you to be proud of the fact that you are married. Marriage is your greatest temporal and spiritual asset. Focus on the strengths that you now have as a married couple as you meet life's challenges and opportunities. Work at making your good marriage even better!

INTERFERENCE

Anything can interfere with your marriage if you allow it to do so. This goes for televisions, cars, computers, children, family members, pets, jobs, hobbies, sports, and even Church callings. Some people solve this problem by actually eliminating whatever it is that interferes. This works to some degree, but some things cannot be eliminated. Would you eliminate your kids? Not hardly! How about your other family members? Are you kidding? Not a chance! Perhaps the job or Church callings? No! Those can't go either. The solution is twofold: *eliminating* things that are unimportant in your life and *emphasizing* those things that are truly important to your life and family relationship.

The key is to control all of the extraneous demands on your time by planning and giving time to only what's truly important. Your relationship with your spouse is one of the most important things of all. So it is important for you to take control, prioritize, and plan to do what's truly important.

FEELING GUILTY ABOUT BEING SEXUAL

Heavenly Father personally gave His children (Adam and Eve) a commandment to multiply and replenish the earth (Gen. 1:28). Having children requires, of course, that man and woman engage in sexual intercourse. Since God commanded men and women to have children, it is obvious that such activity is not evil, dirty, or nasty as long as it is within the bonds of marriage. President Spencer W. Kimball also taught that sex is righteous and that it isn't only for procreation; it is also for showing love to each other and for bonding between husband and wife. President Kimball stated "that God himself implanted the physical magnetism between the sexes for two reasons: for the propagation of the human race, and for the expression of that kind of love between man and wife that makes for true oneness."[16]

Individuals who have been taught during their childhood that sex, either in thought or deed, is dirty, nasty, or unrighteous may have a difficult time after they are married in overcoming those myths. For them it's often difficult to change their negative thinking about sex, even within the bounds of marriage. Somehow, to them, it just doesn't seem like sexual activity could be righteous. Both men and women can share this belief; however, it seems that men more easily dispel these myths than women. When faulty teaching has taken place, and one partner or the other has a difficult time after marriage in thinking of sexual relations as being righteous, it's important to learn to communicate effectively with your partner. Consider consulting your physician, a counselor, or your bishop, and definitely seek advice from your Father in Heaven.

Sometimes concerns and emotions about sex being dirty are so deeply rooted that counseling is required for the couple by one who is trained in sex therapy. Early treatment is easier and usually more effective than later treatment. If therapy is needed, couples should be counseled together. It's important that the therapist be sensitive to the values of their patients and that he or she not encourage activities that are not consistent with Church standards. It would probably be best to seek help from an LDS therapist, or a therapist who is informed about and sensitive to LDS theology, so that the couple can be assured that the counselor understands gospel principles.

Attempts to Use Unrighteous Dominion

Marriage is a partnership with absolute equality between wife and husband. The righteous exercise of priesthood leadership is a blessing to the family. The Church teaches clearly that an attempt to use the priesthood as a means of enforcing personal preferences, ideas, wants, and desires is unrighteous and sinful. Families are to be led using the principles of order, unity, and agency. Decisions need to be made together with careful consideration of the feelings of both wife and husband.

If the husband who is a priesthood holder abuses that authority, he has used it unrighteously; God then withdraws His approval and in actual effect, such a husband no longer holds the authority to act in God's name even for his own family (D&C 121:37). (A wife must not exercise dominion over her husband either.) Marriage is a true partnership where both husband and wife have equal authority. If the two of them establish their relationship on this basis early in their marriage, they will avoid many difficulties, and they will love and respect each other.

PREVIOUS SEXUAL ABUSE

A national survey of sexual behavior in the United States revealed that sexually forced contacts by adolescents and adults with children are not rare. The researchers found that about 17 percent of adult women and 12 percent of adult men reported that they had been inappropriately sexually touched or mistreated when they were children. Furthermore, only about one in four had told anyone about this experience.[17] Feelings of resentment, violation, terror, and anger toward your spouse because of past sexual abuse or maltreatment by another person can be very damaging to intimacy in marriage. These negative sexual feelings toward the perpetrator can carry over into marriage. Such feelings can make it difficult or impossible to relax, trust, and achieve sexual satisfaction with your spouse. Because of pent-up anger, fear, or resentment that stems from past abuse, these women and men will often have a difficult time responding to their spouse's sexual advances. For them, sexual desire is neither safe nor loving.

While such feelings are understandable, if they're left unresolved they can result in unwarranted bitterness toward the spouse and damage the marriage. Fortunately, counseling is available. Your bishop or a professional therapist can assist in overcoming the effects of past abuse. When a wife (or husband) has been the victim of previous sexual mistreatment or abuse, it is important for both husband and wife to remember that it was the wife or husband who was the victim of this evil act, and that he or she is completely innocent. The victims of the evil acts of others are not guilty of sin.

Underlying Fears of Sex

Other fearful situations aside from previous sexual abuse that are common for many women include a fear of becoming pregnant, fear of infection, or fear of experiencing pain. If fear of pregnancy is the problem for either the wife or husband, discuss this with your physician. There are many ways to effectively prevent pregnancy. (We discuss pregnancy in chapter 9.) If there's significant pain or infection associated with intercourse, it's often a simple problem that can be treated. However, your physician should evaluate frequent and persistent painful intercourse.

Manipulation

Sex should never be used as a tool for manipulating or controlling your spouse. Withholding sex or using sex as a weapon (for revenge, to get even for perceived wrongdoing, or to try to get your spouse to behave a certain way) is a horrible misuse of a God-given gift. It completely breaks the trust necessary for a healthy sexual relationship. A spirit of unselfishness and love should be present with every sexual encounter between you.

In-Laws

Parents and other relatives can sometimes unintentionally undermine a marriage. They may forget that you two are now a family and are, or should be, establishing your own autonomy as a family unit. The Lord has said, "Therefore shall a man leave his father and his mother, and shall cleave unto his wife: and they shall be one flesh" (Gen. 2:24). Your own new family, that is your spouse, should be your first priority.

Years ago President Spencer W. Kimball advised that young married couples live apart from their parents after the wedding. "Couples do well to immediately find their own home, separate and apart from that of the in-laws on either side. The home may be very modest and unpretentious, but still it is an independent domicile. Your married life should become independent of her folks and his folks. You love them more than ever; you cherish their counsels; you appreciate their association; but you live your own lives, being governed by your decisions, by your own prayerful considerations after you have received the counsel from those who should give it."[18] His advice was for couples to live independently, establishing traditions and dealing with trials, all of which make a couple strong as they rely on each other and the Lord. The point is that the newlywed couple needs to establish their independence from their families-of-origin. Of course couples need to define and demonstrate their connections to their larger family networks. It is true that "you don't just marry an individual, you marry a family." Just remember your marriage with your spouse is your top priority; you have created a new family "branch" on the family tree and a distinct family unit in the records of the Church.

TIME CONSTRAINTS AND LACK OF RECREATION

Be careful not to let outside influences prevent you from putting your spouse first—not your job, not your friends, not your parents and family, not your hobbies, not your Church responsibilities. Except for true emergencies, planned time commitments between husbands and wives need to be protected from all other potential interferences. Other people can always replace you at work or at Church. You, however, do not want to have your wife (or husband) replace you! A wife will never believe she's the most important person in a husband's life until he has shown that he's willing to defend his commitments to her against all others.

A story is told of a bishop telling his wife that she was better off second or third on his list than first in some of the marriages he had to counsel. She replied that she would rather be first on someone else's list! Husbands, don't be guilty of making your wife wish she was first on someone else's list. (The same advice applies to wives as well.)

Make certain that some of your planned time together is spent just having fun. Having fun and laughing together deepens your close, loving relationship. Investing a reasonable amount of time and money for recreation isn't a luxury; it's a necessity. If you like doing the same things together, having fun is easy. But what if you like to do different things? The answer is to expand your horizons and your interests. Find new activities that you can both enjoy doing together. Compromising and taking turns are always good and can help you develop new interests. Certainly you did things together before marriage that were mutually enjoyable (unless one or the other of you was faking it). Continue to do those activities and discover some new ones as well.

Lack of Mutual Respect

When one or both partners begin to "expect" rather than to "respect," anger and resentment can begin to build. In a marriage, there are few sins as great as ingratitude and lack of respect. When marriage partners begin to feel they're being taken for granted, they become resentful, which leads to anger. The offending spouse might not even know why his or her spouse is angry. It's extremely important for you to verbalize your appreciation for your spouse. It is also important that you convey nonverbally the same sentiment. Giving hugs, frequently saying "thank you," taking time to listen, and writing notes are just a few examples of how you can express your appreciation. The sin of ingratitude can severely damage a relationship.

Financial Mismanagement

Problems with finances are among the most common of all difficulties that couples face. It isn't the amount of money that's the problem; it's how money is handled. Both partners must feel good about how it is spent or not spent.

There are a few important questions regarding finances that should be resolved early in any relationship. They are: managing the checkbook, deciding what needs to be purchased, discussing where money needs to be spent, and agreeing how and how much to save for future needs and wants. Probably the best thing for a newlywed couple to do is to purchase a good book on family budgeting and financial planning.

One of the most difficult things young couples have to learn about finances is that they need to delay gratification. They can't have what mom and dad have—yet. It took their parents years to acquire their current financial status. The young couple has to work for what they get before they get it. It's much easier to go without when you both have a goal in mind and are working toward that goal. The worst way to sabotage the best plan in the world is for one or both partners to spend more than what they have available. Going into debt for unnecessary items is a sure road to disaster.

One way for couples to keep control of spending is to make two lists: one for *needs* and one for *wants*. One couple started a third list that they called *weeds*. This list was for items that they weren't sure were wants or needs. The couple found that most weeds turned out to be wants and if not carefully managed would choke their financial stability.

We believe that more marriages end because of the couple's inability to handle their finances than for almost any other reason. When there's no money to pay bills and buy needed items such as food and clothing, and when there's no money for the rent, it's hard for either wives or husbands to feel affectionate. Financial worries cause more problems in the bedroom than most young couples realize. The fact is, "Love just ain't enough!" It takes financial responsibility for love to flourish and last.

KEEPING CONFIDENCES AND SEEKING HELP FOR PROBLEMS

As a rule it is best not to discuss details of marital problems or frustrations with those who are emotionally close to you, such as parents or close friends. The reason for this is that these people are usually biased so that they cannot give you, as an individual or as a couple, objective help and insight. Also, these close and personal relationships will continue after you have solved the problems or frustrations of the moment. And while you as a couple have moved beyond or have forgotten the problem, those you asked for advice may have not. You wouldn't want your parents or close friends to think poorly of your spouse for the rest of your marriage. In most cases it is just best not to publically air out your dirty linen.

Having said that, we do not wish to convey that you should not seek appropriate help for serious problems. The two of you should decide together who might be helpful and then seek help as a couple. Such resources might be your bishop, a medical doctor, or a counselor or therapist. These persons might assist you in determining the appropriateness of consulting your parents or involving them in your problem or concern.

EXCESSIVE WORRY

Excessive tensions and worry about life's problems can place a strain on physical relationships even in the best of marriages. However, this is one of the times when a close physical relationship can be really important. A mutually satisfying sexual relationship can unite the couple and give them the additional strength needed to face their current problems.

Chapter Nine

Family Planning

The decisions related to family planning and birth control are among the most important decisions that a married couple will make. Because couples have different backgrounds and expectations they may have different ideas about planning for the birth of their children. Some believe they should leave all decisions to their Heavenly Father or to chance. Others think it is totally up to them to decide. The truth probably lies somewhere in between.

The LDS Church does have a "policy" on birth control, which is found in the *Handbook of Instructions for Bishoprics and Stake Presidencies.* In the handbook it states that it is a privilege for couples to have children and that the couple then is responsible to nurture and rear them. The decision as to how many children to have and when to have them is personal and private and is for the couple to decide. The statement admonishes couples not to judge one another in such matters. It also points out that sexual relations in marriage are divinely approved and are a means for procreation and for expressing love and strengthening emotional and spiritual bonding between the husband and wife.

If you have questions about the Church's policy on birth control, you should make an appointment with your bishop to talk about this important issue. (The bishop will most likely appreciate your questions and give you helpful advice and information on other marital topics too.) Then make it a matter of fasting and prayer as you reach the decision that is right for you.

Before your wedding is the best time to obtain information on birth control. This can be done during the premarital exam. Then, should the two of you wish to plan for and obtain birth control medication or supplies, you can do it prior to the wedding night. After you have received medical advice regarding the types of birth control available, the decision about the best method to be used, and when to discontinue birth control and begin your family is a personal decision that only you and your spouse can make.

To help you in your decisions, the remainder of this chapter presents basic information regarding how best to become pregnant, as well as basic information regarding pregnancy prevention. The information here is very limited, and we strongly recommend that you obtain additional information from your personal physician.

THE MENSTRUAL CYCLE AND FERTILITY

In order to understand how different birth control methods work, it helps to understand how a woman's menstrual cycle works. An average menstrual cycle lasts about 28 days. During the first half of the cycle, the brain and pituitary gland stimulate the ovaries to produce estrogen and stimulate eggs to mature and become ready to be released by the ovary. Around day 14 from the first day of menstrual flow, the pituitary gland releases a surge of a hormone called luteinizing hormone (LH) which causes the egg to be released from the ovary (ovulation) and picked up by the fallopian tube. Here fertilization takes place if there are sperm present from recent intercourse. The fertilized egg then travels down the tube to the uterus where it implants in the lining of the uterus (endometrium) and grows into a baby.

After the egg is released from the ovary, during the second two weeks of the cycle, the ovary continues to make estrogen but also makes another hormone called progesterone. If the egg is not fertilized, estrogen and progesterone levels start to decrease about two weeks after ovulation, and this drop in hormone levels causes the lining of the uterus to be shed. This is the start of the woman's next menstrual period. At the same time, the brain begins stimulating a new egg to mature and starts the cycle over again.

Getting Pregnant: Finding Your Fertile Period

There are several ways of determining when a woman is ovulating. If her cycles are very regular (always 28 or 30 or 33 days, for example), it can be a simple matter of watching the calendar. The time from the start of the period to ovulation is the part that makes cycles longer or shorter. The next period comes very reliably 14 days after ovulation. For example, if you have 28-day cycles you probably ovulate on day 14, but if you have 33-day cycles you probably ovulate on day 19.

For women with more variable cycles, there are other methods. Many women notice a change in their cervical mucus, which becomes more clear and stringy and more abundant around the time of ovulation. There are urine test strips (somewhat like a pregnancy test), which detect the LH surge, that you can purchase at most pharmacies. Once the LH surge is detected, ovulation occurs approximately 36 hours later. You can also keep a basal body temperature chart, which is a graph of your temperature (taken before getting out of bed in the morning) every day of your cycle. Because of the hormone progesterone, the basal body temperature increases about one-half degree Fahrenheit around the time of ovulation and stays up for the second half of the cycle.

Once the time of ovulation is determined, pregnancy is best achieved by having intercourse on the day of and for three to four days prior to ovulation. Intercourse at least every other day during this period will maximize your chances for conception.

When you do decide to attempt pregnancy, it is important for the woman to begin taking a prenatal vitamin or at least a folic acid supplement one to three months before conceiving. Folic acid (or folate) is a B vitamin that helps prevent spina bifida, a serious birth defect of the spinal cord and brain that can form in the very early weeks of pregnancy, possibly even before you know you are pregnant. You need at least 400 micrograms (0.4 milligrams) of folate daily prior to pregnancy and at least 800 micrograms (0.8 mg) during pregnancy. This is more than twice the recommended daily allowance for men and nonpregnant women.

Other studies suggest that supplements derived from fish oil, omega-3 fatty acids, are also beneficial. They may improve fetal brain and eye development as well as decreasing certain complications associated with pregnancy. Calcium and vitamin D are also important. Four to six servings of dairy products is sufficient. Supplements can also be taken to help achieve adequate calcium intake.

CONTRACEPTION

There is no perfect method of birth control. All methods can have side effects and all can fail to prevent pregnancy, even permanent sterilization. The only way to prevent pregnancy 100 percent is to not have sex (abstinence). Abstinence is also the only way to prevent sexually transmitted diseases (STDs) 100 percent. However, some methods are more effective than others in preventing pregnancy and STDs. In the following discussion, if we say a method has a 5 percent failure rate, that means if 100 women use that method for a year, 5 will become pregnant. Failure rates are higher if the contraceptive method is not used perfectly.

There are four general categories of birth control. They are:

1. Natural Methods
2. Barrier Methods
3. IUD (Intrauterine Device)
4. Hormonal Methods

NATURAL METHODS

Natural methods for birth control include breast feeding, natural planning, and withdrawal. All of these methods have a high failure rate. The chance of becoming pregnant within the year while using any of these natural methods is around 15 percent.

Breast-feeding

This is the most common form of birth control used around the world. When a woman breast-feeds, a hormone called prolactin is released from her pituitary gland in the brain. This hormone decreases (not eliminates) the chance of becoming pregnant by suppressing ovulation. For breast-feeding to be somewhat effective as a contraceptive method the infant must be breast-fed at least 4–6 times each day.

If a woman exclusively breast-feeds for the first six months and has no periods, there is a less than 2 percent chance she will become pregnant. However, after the first six months or if she has periods during the first six months, the failure rate is much higher.

Natural Planning

This is also known as the rhythm method or periodic abstinence. This method relies on the fact that pregnancy can only occur on the day of ovulation and up to four days prior. Thus, to practice this type of birth control you must be able to predict the time of ovulation. To be able to do this accurately a woman must be very regular with her menstrual cycle. Ovulation occurs 14 days prior to the next period, but the time from the period to ovulation can be very variable. Checking cervical mucus and your daily morning temperature can aid in determining when ovulation is about to or has occurred, but these things are not as useful because by the time ovulation is detected, there can still be a pregnancy from intercourse up to three days before. Further, a woman can ovulate later than expected, even when she is usually very regular. The failure rate for this method is unacceptably high for most women, between 3 to 20 percent, depending on the regularity of cycles and how strictly intercourse is avoided in the fertile period.

Withdrawal

With this method the husband attempts to withdraw prior to ejaculation. However, a small amount of fluid containing sperm is often released during arousal and foreplay. This small amount can cause pregnancy. In addition, if the husband pulls out too late, pregnancy can obviously occur. The overall failure rate is between 5 to 25 percent.

Barrier Methods

Barrier methods include condoms, spermicides, and the diaphragm. The cervical cap is a barrier method similar to a diaphragm that has been commonly used in Europe, but is not currently available in the United States.

Spermicides

Spermicides are chemicals that kill sperm. Foams, gels, suppositories, sponges, and vaginal contraceptive film are available at most pharmacies and drugstores. All contain the same spermicide, nonoxynol-9. They are placed in the vagina prior to each episode of intercourse. Spermicides should not be used alone as a method of birth control because failure rates range from 10 to 40 percent.

Condoms

The breakage and leakage rates for condoms are approximately 15 percent with pregnancy rates of 3 to 15 percent. Therefore, those couples who really want to avoid pregnancy should use an additional form of birth control. The combination of spermicide and condoms provides very good protection with failure rates of 2 to 4 percent.

Diaphragm

The diaphragm is a flexible rubber disk that is inserted into the vagina and rests behind the pubic bone. Spermicide must be used with this method because the diaphragm does not form a tight seal; the diaphragm functions properly by holding the spermicide against the cervix. The diaphragm can be inserted up to six hours before intercourse. In addition, the diaphragm should be removed between 6–24 hours after each episode of intercourse and cleaned. Its failure rate is 6 to 12 percent. It also must fitted by a physician. Because of all of these limitations, the diaphragm is not used as much today as is once was.

IUD (INTRAUTERINE DEVICE)

The IUD is one of the most effective forms of birth control with failure rates of less than 1 percent. It is the most commonly used reversible birth control method in the world but is less popular in the United States. IUDs are small T-shaped devices that fit inside the uterus, remain in place, and are effective for up to 10 years, depending on the type of IUD. It prevents pregnancies by changing the consistency of the cervical mucus so that sperm cannot get through and by causing an inflammatory reaction in the lining of the uterus that kills sperm if they do get through. Few, if any sperm get into the fallopian tubes. Unfortunately, many women elect not to use this form of birth control because they mistakenly believe that IUDs work by preventing a fertilized egg from implanting inside the uterus. However, the IUD's principal mechanism of action is preventing sperm from getting to the egg.

The IUD is placed in position by a physician during an office examination that is similar to having a pap smear. Inserting the IUD does cause some cramping or discomfort for many women, but this is brief and usually not severe. Removal is also easily done in the doctor's office, and a woman's ability to get pregnant returns within one to two months.

Advantages of the IUD include low failure rate, convenience, and freedom from hormonal side effects. The main disadvantage with the IUD is its effect on the menstrual cycle. Some IUDs can cause heavier, more painful periods, mainly in the first few months. However, newer IUDs which release low levels of the hormone progesterone can actually decrease or even stop menstrual bleeding.

In the 1970s, an older type of IUD was used which caused severe pelvic infections that sometimes led to infertility. The IUDs on the market today do not carry those same risks. However, if a woman is infected with chlamydia or gonorrhea at the time an IUD is inserted, it can lead to a more serious pelvic infection. For this reason, some doctors require a chlamydia test before inserting an IUD. Women in mutually faithful relationships have very little risk of pelvic infection with IUDs.

Hormonal Methods

Hormonal methods include oral contraceptives (pills), the patch, the ring, and Depo-Provera injections. Each method works differently to prevent pregnancy.

Oral Contraception

Oral contraception, also known as birth control pills ("the pill"), is the most common form of reversible contraception used in the United States today. There are two general types: combination pills and progesterone-only pills.

Combination Birth Control Pill

This is the most common pill used. The combination pill contains both estrogen and progesterone (see "The Menstrual Cycle and Fertility" earlier in this chapter). The combination birth control pill suppresses ovulation, thickens cervical mucus, and thins the lining of the uterus. When taken as directed, all brands of combination birth control pills are equally effective with failure rates at about 1 to 6 percent, depending on how consistently they are used. You need a prescription for birth control pills, so if you choose this option you must first consult your physician.

The pill should be taken every day. However, if only one day is missed, protection is still good but two pills should be taken the next day. If three days are missed, you should take one pill on the third day, but you should use other forms of birth control for the remainder of the month. To help remind patients, many physicians advise their patients to take their pill when they brush their teeth—although the pill can be taken at any time during the day. However, some women get a little nauseated with the pill and find that taking it just prior to going to bed is helpful.

Most women tolerate the pill very well. The most common side effects that occur include nausea, headache, emotional irritability, and/or light bleeding between periods, especially during the first month or two. These side effects, if present, usually decrease over a few months as the body adjusts to them. They may be reduced or eliminated by switching to a different brand of pill.

Birth control pills are very safe for healthy women. However, you should not take the pill if you may currently be pregnant or if you have ever had a stroke, heart attack, breast cancer, or a blood clot in the lungs or leg. You should also not use the pill if you are over 35 years old and use tobacco. If a parent or sibling has had a blood clot or stroke you should tell your doctor before taking oral contraceptives. He or she may want to run some blood tests prior to having you start the pill.

For women without those health problems, birth control pills actually have many health benefits. Periods may be lighter and less painful. Further, taking the pill may lessen the possibility of anemia, ovarian and uterine cancer, ovarian cysts, endometriosis, and problems with acne.

Two major advantages of this form of contraception are that it will regulate a woman's menstrual cycle, and it usually helps decrease both menstrual cramping and menstrual blood flow. In addition, it is possible to alter when the period is going to occur. Most brides-to-be do not schedule their wedding and honeymoon around their period. The ability to delay the period several weeks, until the honeymoon is over, for many is a lifesaver. In order to do this, however, the pill must be started several months prior to the wedding.

Progesterone-Only Birth Control Pill

The progesterone-only pill, or "mini pill" contains no estrogen and only about one-fourth the progesterone found in combination pills. It works by thickening the cervical mucus and thinning the lining of the uterus, but does not always prevent release of eggs from the ovaries. This pill must be taken every day and, importantly, at the same time each day. Failure rates are 1 to 9 percent depending on consistency of use. About half of the women who take this pill have irregular periods. For women who are not able to use estrogen it is a very good option.

However, the most common reason women use this pill is because they are breast-feeding. The estrogen in the combination pill does not negatively affect the baby, though it can have a negative effect on mother's milk supply.

The Patch and the Ring

These are two newer forms of birth control that work exactly like the combination birth control pill except the estrogen and progesterone are absorbed by your body instead of taken orally. The patch is placed on the skin and changed weekly. It allows the hormones to be absorbed directly through the skin. The ring is a small plastic ring that is placed in the vagina and stays in for three weeks at a time. The hormones are absorbed through the skin of the vagina. It does not need to be removed for intercourse and most women cannot feel it when it is in place. Both of these methods have advantages, disadvantages, and health effects similar to birth control pills, but they can be much more convenient, especially for women who have difficulty remembering to take pills. Like the pill, these methods require a doctor's prescription.

Depo-Provera Injection

Depo-Provera ("the shot") is an injection given every three months at your doctor's office. It contains a progesterone-like hormone and works by keeping the ovaries from releasing eggs and thickening the cervical mucus to keep sperm from reaching the eggs. It is one of the most effective reversible methods of birth control, with failure rates between 0.3 percent to 3 percent depending on consistency of use. Protection is immediate if you get the shot during the first five days of your period. Otherwise, you will need an additional method of contraception for the first two weeks.

Depo-Provera can cause unpredictable but usually light menstrual bleeding. Up to 70 percent of women have irregular bleeding during the first year but this statistic decreases to less than 10 percent by the second year, and, in fact, after two years of use, 70 percent of women have no periods at all. One possible but significant drawback to this method is that it can take up to a year after the last Depo shot to get pregnant.

PERMANENT STERILIZATION

Church members considering this serious step should consult with their bishop regarding the Church's guidelines in this matter. Minor surgery to permanently prevent pregnancy can be performed on either men, (vasectomy) or women (tubal ligation). Failure rates for tubal ligation and vasectomy are both around 0.5 percent.

A vasectomy can be performed in a physician's office under local anesthetic. After a vasectomy, other forms of birth control must be used for three to four months because a man has about a three-month reserve of sperm. A semen analysis should be done three months after the vasectomy to ensure that sterilization has occurred.

A tubal ligation is a same-day surgery performed in a hospital or surgical center using clips, electricity (electrocautery), or by removing a section of the fallopian tube. The failure rates differ with each method as do the rates of reversal success. Tubal ligation is often done immediately after delivery of a baby. If an epidural is used during labor, the anesthetic can be continued and used for the tubal ligation as well. Once a woman has recovered from her tubal ligation, protection from pregnancy is immediate. If pregnancy does occur after a tubal ligation, there is a much higher chance of an ectopic pregnancy (a fertilized egg developing in the fallopian tube rather than in the uterus). This can be a life-threatening condition if not treated immediately.

While both vasectomy and tubal ligation can be reversed, reversals are (1) expensive, (2) not covered by insurance, and (3) not always successfully reversed. Reversing a vasectomy is less successful than reversing a tubal ligation.

Infertility

When married couples are unable to achieve a pregnancy it can be emotionally devastating. Arms ache to hold a newborn. Deep emotional pain is felt every time close friends and family members announce a new pregnancy, and tears are shed with the arrival of each menstrual period. Unfortunately, this isn't an uncommon problem. Ten to fifteen percent of all couples experience difficulties in becoming pregnant. This year, over one million women will seek treatment for infertility, and this number is increasing. Often treatment is simple and inexpensive, but if advanced reproduction techniques are needed such as in vitro fertilization (IVF), costs can soar as high as $10,000 to $15,000 each cycle with only about a 40 to 60 percent chance of success.

Infertility is not just a female problem. Forty percent of the time it is the wife who is subfertile, 30–40 percent of the time it is the husband who has the problem, and up to 20 percent of the time it is both partners who have something wrong. Because of the high percentage of both partners having a problem, both should always be tested.

Unfortunately even when extensive testing is performed, 15 to 20 percent of the time no problem is found. This is termed "unexplained infertility."

It is important for couples who feel they are having difficulties becoming pregnant to have a basic understanding of normal pregnancy rates. If the circumstances are right, most mammals have an 80 percent chance of becoming pregnant each month. Humans, on the other hand, have only a 20 percent chance of becoming pregnant in a given month. The medical term for pregnancies per month is fecundity rate. Because humans only have a 20 percent fecundity rate, it takes one full year before 85 to 90 percent of couples trying to become pregnant will be so. This is why most reproductive specialists recommend waiting for one full year before seeking treatment. The only exceptions are those couples who know they have a specific problem or women who rarely menstruate.

Every couple undergoing evaluation and treatment for infertility should have a semen analysis done, confirmation of ovulation, and a test where fluid or dye is pushed through the uterus and out the fallopian tubes to ensure the tubes are open. There are a number of ways to confirm ovulation and to evaluate the fallopian tubes.

The most frequent problems affecting fertility rates are:

1. *Low semen count, volume, or motility,* which can sometimes be corrected with surgery. Often this problem requires in vitro fertilization or artificial insemination.

2. *Irregular ovulation,* which often results from hormonal problems with the thyroid, adrenal, or pituitary glands. Medications can be used to correct hormonal imbalances or to stimulate production of eggs.

3. *Endometriosis,* which is tissue from inside the uterus that gets outside and implants in the pelvis. This can often be treated with surgery or medications.

4. *Scar tissue,* which is usually due to previous infections, endometriosis, or pelvic surgery. This can often be treated with surgery or in vitro fertilization.

Additional discussion regarding evaluation and treatment for infertility is beyond the scope of this book. Those couples who have not been able to conceive after trying for one year should see a specialist who is experienced in both the evaluation and treatment of infertility.

Chapter Ten

Frequently Asked Questions

IS PERSONAL PRIVACY IMPORTANT NOW THAT WE ARE MARRIED?

Yes. Respect for each other's privacy is and will always be important. Even after marriage, people need privacy for reasons beyond their bodily functions. A certain amount of "space" is required for all individuals to feel secure with themselves. If you don't feel secure with yourself, it's impossible to feel secure with your spouse. You can smother your partner if you don't allow him or her the space and time alone that he or she may need. Individuals need different amounts of privacy and space. Individual upbringing is a major factor in how much time and space you will need, as well as how you react to your spouse's need for privacy. Those who come from small families where privacy was not an issue because family members could be alone when they wanted require more space and privacy than those who come from large families where it was difficult to be alone. It is important to recognize these differences and allow time to make appropriate adjustments.

IS IT NORMAL FOR THE HUSBAND TO CLIMAX BEFORE HIS WIFE?

Yes. In fact the idea of simultaneous husband-and-wife orgasm is much more a myth than reality. Through sexual intercourse alone, a husband will reach orgasm much sooner than his wife. The term "premature" or "early ejaculation" describes what is happening and is not usually a medical disorder. However, it can be a frustration. Early ejaculation can be expected during first sexual experiences, often occurring on the honeymoon or initial attempts at intercourse. Sexually speaking, premature ejaculators are okay in every way except that they simply come (reach orgasm) too fast. This problem subsides as the couple becomes sexually experienced and the newness of sexual interaction subsides.

I Have No Interest in Having Sex. What Is Wrong with Me?

Sexual dysfunction and problems can be broadly categorized as decreased interest, decreased sexual response, or the inability to achieve a climax. Most commonly, women complain of decreased interest, but men do too. The medical term is "decreased libido." This problem can be related to a number of factors including such things as fatigue, lack of time, depression, relationship problems, or stress. Rarely is decreased libido related to hormonal problems.

To help resolve this problem, it is necessary to find (capture) time to reestablish your emotional and physical relationship with each other. Regaining and then maintaining a healthy marital relationship (see chapters 11 and 12) will more than likely increase your interest in sex. If hormones or depression are the problem, being evaluated by your doctor and taking medicine if he or she prescribes it will boost an emotionally healthy relationship, which can set you on the path to a sexually satisfying one.

Is Painful Intercourse Normal?

No. However, when a woman first begins sexual activity there will be pain as the hymen (opening to the vagina) is stretched. However, the pain should rapidly decrease. After the initial stretching has occurred, a woman should not experience pain when having sexual relations. If she continues to have pain, she should be seen by her physician.

There are two broad types of painful intercourse. Neither is normal. First, there is pain at the vaginal opening or just inside the vagina. This may be caused by lack of lubrication or attempting to penetrate too early (not enough foreplay). However, this is often related to other causes, some of which are difficult to treat. If inadequate foreplay is not the problem, you should be seen by your doctor. Second, pain that is deep (like something being hit) is never normal, and if it occurs frequently or is severe, it should be investigated immediately.

Is Bleeding after Intercourse Normal?

Usually yes. The cervix can sometimes bleed when touched. This is particularly true during pregnancy. So pregnant or not, light bleeding after intercourse doesn't normally indicate there is a problem. However, if you are not pregnant and bleed heavily after intercourse, you should see a doctor. It may be related to a significant cervical abnormality.

As mentioned above, if you are pregnant, a small amount of bleeding after intercourse can be normal. However, bleeding that persists or increases may be more serious. Bleeding early in pregnancy may be a sign of ectopic pregnancy or miscarriage. Bleeding later in pregnancy may be a symptom of preterm labor with cervical dilation or a separation of the placenta from the uterus (placental abruption). All of these conditions can be serious. You should call your physician if you have bleeding that is more than a few spots.

Do Antidepressants Affect My Sexual Response?

Yes! While it is sometimes difficult to determine if decreased sexual response is related to being depressed or to the antidepressants, most of the newer medications have a negative impact on sexual response. Antidepressants can make it much more difficult to climax. For men who have problems with premature ejaculation, this is beneficial. But for women, many of whom already have difficulty climaxing, this can be problematic.

Except indirectly, antidepressants should not have a negative effect on sexual interest. If this is the major problem, it is probably related to the depression itself. On the other hand, if you have decreased interest in sex because of depression, antidepressants may actually *increase* your sexual interest.

Can I Give My Yeast Infection to My Husband?

No, and he cannot give one to you either. Women's yeast infections are usually from the fungal infection *Candida albicans,* though other strains may be involved. Candida, or yeast, is everywhere in the environment, but it prefers dark, warm, moist areas to grow. Fortunately there are natural immunities in a woman's body that help prevent yeast from overgrowing and becoming symptomatic. The fact is, every woman has a small amount of yeast in her vagina, just as everyone has small amounts on his or her skin. When the fungus grows faster than a woman's body can control, a yeast infection develops, causing redness, itching, and burning. Women who find themselves experiencing symptoms consistent with recurrent vaginal yeast infections should be evaluated by their doctor. It may be something entirely different than yeast.

ARE CERTAIN POSITIONS BETTER FOR ACHIEVING PREGNANCY ?

Yes and no. No one position has been shown to be better than another with regard to becoming pregnant. However, research has shown improved pregnancy rates if, after intercourse, a woman lies flat in bed for approximately twenty minutes instead of immediately standing up. Standing on one's head or other unusual body positions do not appear to offer any improvement in pregnancy rates.

HOW OFTEN IS IT NORMAL TO HAVE SEXUAL RELATIONS?

The word *normal* too often implies "healthy." In this discussion we do not use the word *normal* to mean "healthy" or "right." What is "normal" varies from couple to couple. Adjusting to a mutually satisfying frequency of lovemaking is one of the challenges of marriage. Both of you will probably have to make adjustments. The main thing to remember is to put your partner first and try your best to adjust your preferences. However, having said that, it is not abnormal for a couple to engage in sexual intercourse only once a month, nor is it abnormal to have sex once or twice a day. In short, sexual frequency is highly variable and requires understanding, patience, and agreement on the part of both husband and wife. Usually, men desire sex more often than women. Both sexual desire and frequency decrease with age. The average number of sexual encounters for healthy 20- to 40-year-olds is about 2 times a week. Again, this is highly variable.[19] What is important is that both partners are generally comfortable with the sexual frequency in their relationship. Discuss your expectations with each other.

IS IT OKAY TO HAVE SEX DURING PREGNANCY?

There are very few reasons to refrain from sex during pregnancy. If the expectant mother is healthy and has no risk factors associated with her pregnancy, sex will not harm either the mother or her baby. However, if you have problems with preterm labor or are at risk for preterm labor, or have a placenta that overlies the cervix, your doctor will probably suggest that you refrain from sexual relations. Keep in mind that you can engage in mutually satisfying lovemaking that does not include intercourse. This can be a part of your intimate relationship.

If an expectant couple decides it's safe to have intercourse during pregnancy, it's important to know that semen contains prostaglandins, which can stimulate the uterus into having contractions. Also, the hormone oxytocin (which naturally stimulates contractions during childbirth) is released during arousal and orgasm. Therefore, strong contractions with orgasm or some cramping after intercourse is normal. Because semen contains prostaglandins, intercourse in the eighth month may contribute to the starting of labor. If contractions do occur and if they persist for more than two hours, or if contraction pains increase in intensity, you should be evaluated either by your physician or by a nurse at the hospital.

It is also important to know that the cervix bleeds more easily when a woman is pregnant. This is because the elevated estrogen during pregnancy increases the blood flow to the cervix, making the thinner, more fragile inner cervical cells more exposed. Therefore, it's common for pregnant women to have some vaginal spotting after intercourse. If bleeding occurs only after intercourse, is minimal, and doesn't persist, there's no reason for concern. However, bleeding that is equal to or greater than a period, or that lasts longer than several hours after intercourse should be reported to your physician.

As the pregnancy progresses, intercourse will become more uncomfortable. Therefore, the wife should be in complete charge of sexual frequency and position. For additional concerns or questions regarding sex during pregnancy, contact your physician.

What About Sexual Intercourse after Pregnancy?

After giving birth, the time that is required before resuming sexual intercourse depends on the severity of the episiotomy or tearing of the vulva and vagina. Severe lacerations may require six weeks or more for complete healing to occur. As a rule of thumb, most physicians recommend six weeks of abstinence after childbirth. We strongly recommend that the wife be in complete control of when and how sexual intercourse resumes.

Women who have had a cesarean section can sometimes begin having intercourse sooner than those who have given birth vaginally. However, the overall recovery time with a C-section is substantially longer. In addition, the uterus and abdomen will be tender for a much longer time due to abdominal and uterine incisions. Again, the wife should be in control of when sexual relations resume.

Remember though, mutually satisfying lovemaking can take place without intercourse. The husband must exercise appropriate patience and control. If he does so, he will go a long way in building faith and trust between himself and his wife.

Women who breast-feed have lower estrogen levels than women who don't. Therefore, breast-feeding women may experience vaginal dryness and pain upon penetration. This problem can be best resolved by taking more time in foreplay. However, this is a time where lubrication may be required.

What About Sexual Intercourse During a Menstrual Period?

The only medical reason not to have sex during your period is that bloodborne diseases (HIV, hepatitis, syphilis, etc.) are more easily transmitted during this time. Otherwise, except that it's messy, there's no medical reason to refrain from intercourse at this time. In fact, many couples do have sex during this time. Some women say they have a greater desire for sex just before, during, or just after their period. This could very well mean they're less anxious about becoming pregnant at these times and are able to relax and more easily enjoy sex.

Chapter Eleven

Your Marriage As an Eternal Process

Much of this book has focused on the sexual aspects of marriage because sexual intimacy is a very significant part of the marriage relationship. However, it is but one of the many dimensions of your marriage. Therefore, the remainder of this book will be dedicated to discussing the importance of these other dimensions. We are going to present a specific method to guide you in discovering or rediscovering the many facets and strengths of your unique marital relationship.

When Were You Married?

Ask an engaged couple, "When are you getting married?" and they will give you a calendar date of the upcoming wedding. Ask a married couple, "When were you married?" and they (unless memory fails) will tell you something like "June 14" or "December 21." Isn't it interesting that in our everyday language we consider the wedding date to be the beginning of our marriage? What we mean to say when we ask, "When were you married?" is "When was your wedding?"

The wedding is an event. Marriage is a process. The wedding is the legal ceremony, typically conducted in a religious setting that celebrates and sanctions the marriage. However, marriage is not an event, it is a wonderfully complex, multidimensional process. Marriage is a relationship that is formed and functions over time in multiple dimensions and on many levels.

To say then that marriage begins with the wedding is inaccurate. It is more helpful to view marriage as having begun before the wedding. There is a process that is called premarital courtship that consists of getting to know one another, bonding, and forming a relationship. A more descriptive term for this process is *psychological marriage.*[20] Your psychological marriage began on a private and subtle level as you were dating. It continued forming through your courtship and engagement. And it continues to form, in fact, throughout time and eternity.

THE BONDING PROCESS OF MARRIAGE

We have suggested that marriage is a unique interpersonal relationship. Not only are there strong forces that draw individuals toward each other before marriage, but these same forces function as a kind of gravitational force in marriage. Marriage is a unique form of bonding, held together by those strong forces, e.g. mutual attraction, spirituality, ambition, compassion, work ethic, sexual chemistry, etc.

In most relationships, for most couples, we believe that the bonding process follows a particular progression. Bonding begins privately and individually for each of you during your dating relationship. You took your first step toward bonding when each of you decided, "That person is for me."

The second step you took in the bonding process was interactional. At some point after the first step, each of you began to indicate, verbally and nonverbally, that you held the other person in special regard. This rarely takes place at one point in time, but is a process. And in some sense, and in some way, each of you said to the other, "You are for me." By this time you were already deep in the bonding process, and your relationship had already connected on many levels.

As the bonding solidified, you finally made the third step. As a last declaration, you as a couple, announced to the world what had already happened to you privately and secretly together. When you announced your engagement and had the wedding ceremony, you declared that the bonding was set, even though you were, psychologically speaking, already married.

YOUR MARITAL ROAD MAP

Growing up each of us develops ideas about who we are, what is important to us, and what we expect out of life. At some point, and at some level, we begin to think about what marriage might be like. We begin to consider what sort of person we want to marry. Ideas about our future spouse's characteristics may become part of our dreams and thoughts. Another set of ideas may be related to what it will be like to be married. Less often, but just as important, is the question, "What will I be like as a spouse?" Such ideas and questions should become the beginning of your marital road map.

It can be an enjoyable and useful journey to travel back in time and look at your relationship history—or your "courtship" road map—and journey to your present location. During this journey down memory lane you will discover or rediscover some things about how your relationship has grown and developed psychologically. You will see some of the qualities and characteristics of you, your partner, and your relationship now and over time.

How has your relationship developed and changed? If we think of your relationship history as traveling along a road, what has been the terrain of the road? How have you, individually and together, handled the journey? Have you, or if necessary can you, modify you marriage vehicle (relationship) and road map a bit so that things will be even better?

Research and clinical evidence suggest that a key to successful marriage is flexibility, the ability to adapt and adjust to change. Good marriages, like good cars, need shock absorbers that work well. Take a drive along your road to marriage.

Recalling your relationship history should be a mutual discussion of your recollections, thoughts, feelings, and events as you remember them. You are the experts! The differences between your recollection of events, thoughts, and feelings can be humorous and insightful.

The following section lists questions that can guide you in discussing your relationship history. Some questions ask you to recall events. Others ask you to discuss thoughts or feelings. As you discuss these questions, you will create a time line of your relationship that can be the foundation or review of traveling the road together.

You may wish to write down some responses. Some couples have found it useful to write the topical headings listed below on the side of a page, and at the top of the page make two columns, one for his recollections and one for her recollections. These brief notes can then become reference points for later discussions. You might set up your page to look something like this:

	JAMES	JENNIFER
First Meeting:	*I remember, it was . . .*	*Yes, that was it, BUT I remember that . . .*
First Impressions:	*Wow! You swept me . . .*	*Your roommate really impressed me more at first . . .*
Second Date:	*I hope you were attracted . . .*	*I wondered if you liked me . . .*

(And so on . . .)

Courtship—The First Miles

Begin by looking at when you first met. Remember, this is to be an easy and fun dialogue between the two of you. The discussion could go on for hours and hours! You may discuss this over several days or conversations. Don't be concerned about the time that it takes; rather have fun sharing your recollections and thoughts with each other. Also, the questions listed here are only suggestions. You can add your own questions as they come to mind.

First Meeting

- When did the two of you meet? What year was it?
- How old were each of you at the time?
- How did you first meet? Did you know who the other one was before you met?
- Who introduced you?
- What do you remember about that first meeting?

First Impressions

- After you got back from that first meeting (date), if you had a best friend to whom you would have told everything, and he or she had asked, "What did you think of John or Mary?" what would you have said?
- What did you like about each other?
- What attracted you to each other?
- What did you discover about each other that was different, unusual, or unexpected?

Second Date

- How long after the first meeting or date did the second date occur?
- Who initiated it? How did that happen?
- What were your feelings about seeing each other again?
- Where did you go and how did you decide what you were going to do on the date?

Second Impressions

- At the end of the second date, what do you think that your partner found attractive about you?
- What did you find attractive (interesting) about each other?
- Did you discover anything that was unexpected or different than during the first date?

Exclusivity and Inclusivity

- Did you continue to date others? Did the two of you discuss dating others?
- When did you decide to stop dating others? If you stopped dating others without discussing it, when did you begin to know or sense that the other person was no longer interested in dating other people?
- If you discussed it and decided not to date other people, how did that discussion go?

Friends' and Family's Responses

- How did your friends respond to your dating the other person?
- What did they like about him or her?
- What did they dislike about him or her?
- If family members met the other person, what were their reactions?
- What were your responses to meeting his or her family?

Steady Dating

- When did you each see yourself as going together or as "going steady" or as being "a couple"?
- How did you arrive at this decision? Did you discuss it or did it just happen?
- What did your friends think of your commitment to go steady?

- What did your parents and siblings think about your decision to go steady?

Bonding Process

- When did you say to yourself "He (or she) is for me!" or "He (or she) is someone I'd marry"? (This can be seen as the point of internal commitment, commitment to yourself.)
- When did you begin to say to your partner, "You're for me," or "I could see us getting married?" (This can be seen as the point of external commitment, commitment to your partner but a secret to others.)

Separations

- When the two of you were separated for a while (such as summer, mission, etc.), what did you say to each other about the relationship?
- Where did you think the other person was in regard to the relationship?
- How would you each describe your relationship as you separated?
- What did you do to maintain or cool the relationship during your time apart?

Engagement

- Did you discuss getting engaged?
- Who initiated the discussion?
- When did you discuss getting engaged? What do you recall about those discussions?
- Did you together discuss and shop for an engagement or wedding ring?
- Was the engagement, or "popping the question," a surprise?
- Did you inform your parents or request their permission or blessing of the coming engagement?

- What were your parents' and siblings' reactions when you became engaged?
- How did you see each other's family as reacting to the engagement?
- When and how did you announce your engagement?

Wedding Planning

- How did (will) your wedding plans develop?
- Who was (will) be involved in the wedding planning? What are (were) their roles?
- What did (will) you learn about yourself, each other, and each other's family during the prewedding planning?
- How did each of you experience the wedding? (How do you think you will experience the wedding?)
- How did you decide about a honeymoon?

YOUR MARITAL "VEHICLE"

Up to this point you have been traveling a somewhat traditional and maybe even predictable road to marriage. Hopefully, you have enjoyed and benefitted from your recollections. Now, let's look at some of the dimensions and processes of traveling along the marital road. Think of these as the workings or engine of your marriage vehicle.

Communication

- How would you describe your communication now?
- How has your communication changed over the course of your relationship?
- How do each of you know if you say or do something that pleases the other?
- How do each of you know if you say or do something that the other doesn't like?
- In what ways are you able to express your feelings to the other?

- How do you show your partner that you understand him or her?
- How do you know that your partner understands you?

Caring and Support

- How do you know that your partner cares about you?
- In what ways do you show respect for each other?
- What does your partner do that makes you feel respected?
- How does your partner let you know you are cherished by him or her?
- Have there been times when you feel that you have been taken for granted by your partner?

Personality Issues

- How would you describe your personality?
- How would you describe your partner's personality?
- Are there aspects of your or your partner's personality that you would like to change?
- In what ways are your personalities complementary?
- In what ways are your personalities different?

Conflict

- Do either or both of you avoid conflict with one another?
- How often do you disagree?
- Do you have any arguments?
- What issues or concerns cause arguments?
- How did you make sense of those arguments?
- How were the arguments resolved?
- Who initiated the making-up or peacemaking effort? What was done?
- What was your relationship like after you made up?

Family of origin

- Do you perceive that any family members have interfered with your relationship? If so, how have you handled that?
- Are one or both of you too involved with your family?
- In what way are your (and your partner's) handling of frustrations similar to that of your (and his or her) father?
- In what way are your (and your partner's) handling of frustrations similar to that of your (and his or her) mother?
- In what way are your (and your partner's) giving and receiving of affection similar to that of your (and his or her) father?
- In what way are your (and your partner's) giving and receiving of affection similar to that of your (and his or her) mother?
- Which traits of your parents and their marital relationship do you want to carry into your marriage?
- Which traits might you like to exclude from your marriage?
- What are your impressions of sisters and brothers and sisters- and brothers-in-law?
- Which family members are you most likely to be closest to and relate best to as a couple (now and in the future)?

Social Life

- How do the two of you handle your social life?
- Who is in charge of your social calendar? Do one or both of you initiate ideas regarding your social life?
- Do each of you have friends apart from the other person? Were some friends dropped along the way?
- When, as a couple, did the two of you begin to establish friends who were not known to each of you individually before you started seeing each other?

Leisure Activities

- Do you feel that you have a balance between activities done separately and together?

- What sort of struggles have you had over expectations of having a good time?
- How do you decide what to do together, and separately, for leisure activities?
- Do you share the same sense of what "having fun" means?
- Does one pressure the other to enjoy certain activities?
- Sometimes partners feel that mates are either too busy or too inactive. In what ways is this the case for you two?

Finances

- What have you done to work out a means of handling finances (budget or project income and expenses)?
- How do (will) you share in financial decisions?
- In what ways are your spending and saving habits and expectations similar or different?
- Did you bring (are you bringing) financial debt into the marriage? What is your plan to deal with that?
- What sort of health insurance do (will) you have? (Have you taken care of any preexisting medical or dental problems before the wedding—maybe while on your parents' insurance?)

Intimacy

- In what ways do you feel intimate with (close to) your partner?
- How do you know that you have a private and trusting relationship?
- Are you aware of and responsive to your partner's feelings and sense of well-being?
- Couples are intimate emotionally, physically, spiritually, and cognitively (planning for the future), and in other ways. In what ways is your relationship intimate?
- Which areas in intimacy would you like to increase?

Affection

- How do you demonstrate affection for your partner?
- What are your expectations about giving and receiving affection for your relationship, now and in the future?
- How was (is) affection demonstrated in your family of origin?
- How do you see the differences between affection and sex?

Sexuality

- Is your sex education and knowledge adequate?
- Are your individual attitudes about sex sound and healthy?
- Have you together discussed sexuality and sexual issues and information to the degree that you feel appropriate for your relationship?
- Discuss what the statement, "Being sexual is only one way of being affectionate" means to you.
- Discuss the statement, "Sexual relations within marriage are important not only for the purpose of procreation, but also as a means of expressing love and strengthening emotional and spiritual bonds between husband and wife."

Parenting

- What are your hopes about being parents?
- Have you discussed family planning—the responsibility to nurture and rear children?
- Have you discussed birth control?
- What aspects of parenting from your childhood do you want for your children?

Religious Practice

- In what ways are your religious values a foundation for your relationship and marriage?
- How do (will) you practice your religion in your relationship?

- What are your expectations of your spouse as to religious practice and behavior in your marriage?
- What are your expectations regarding such things as attendance at Church meetings, tithing, fulfilling Church callings, family home evenings, date night, prayer, etc.?

The goal of your dialoguing, reading, and discussing these questions as a couple was to show you the "glue" that binds the two of you together. Such questions can lead you to clarify your individual and couple expectations for your marriage. Hopefully you generated additional questions and discussion on your own too.

While there are common themes across marriages, it is the unique ways that each couple generates the road map and travels through their marriage that is the key to happiness and success. We hope that as you have read, thought about, and discussed the above questions, you will have an impressive inventory of the many important dimensions of your relationship.

A Relationship Questionnaire: Computerized Appraisal

In addition to the self-appraisal dialogue that you have just completed, there is another means of gaining information about your relationship. Many couples have found it useful to take a questionnaire that was specifically designed to provide information about their relationship. The advantage of a questionnaire is that it organizes your responses to questions into scales and charts that show how you compare with each other in many important areas of marriage. Such information can help you understand your expectations about being married and provide you with great information and ideas to discuss together.

An excellent questionnaire for this purpose is RELATE.[21] The name *RELATE* stands for **RELAT**ionship **E**valuation. RELATE is an inventory designed for couples who are dating, thinking about marriage, engaged, or married. It assesses four major areas of the relationship: (1) personality characteristics and values, (2) relationship support from family and friends, (3) communication and conflict resolution skills, and (4) family background.

RELATE will not predict whether your relationship will last or tell you if your relationship is good or bad. What RELATE does is give you information so that you can clarify and evaluate certain aspects, thoughts, and opinions about your relationship. The unique aspect of RELATE is that it is designed to be self-interpreted by the individuals and couples taking it. This is done by providing the RELATE Report directly to the couple for their interpretation and use, which they print out on their own.

The partners take RELATE separately online. After both have completed the questionnaire, the computer immediately prepares the RELATE Report which organizes and provides information from their inventory responses. The RELATE Report shows the couple how they compare to one another using their individual responses to 271 items. It organizes their responses in scales, graphs, and charts and provides guidelines and questions that steer the couple in interpreting and understanding their report. Information from the RELATE questionnaire doesn't tell couples what to do about their relationship, rather it gives them additional information for discussion and planning.

RELATE was developed by researchers and clinicians in a process spanning over 20 years of research and development. The newest version of RELATE, released in 1997, has been taken by more than 45,000 individuals. RELATE is available over the Internet at **www.relate-institute.org**. The cost is 20 dollars per couple or 10 dollars for an individual.

SUMMARY

In this chapter we have provided you with a means of looking at your relationship. As you have traveled through your relationship history and down memory lane, you have had the opportunity to see how your relationship has grown and developed. The purpose of this exercise was to help you become more aware of what you believe about your relationship, how you interact, and how you and your partner affect one another. Also, you may have detected patterns in the ways that you interact. We hope that by doing these things you can strengthen your marriage, making your road to eternal life a happy one.

Chapter Twelve

Keeping Your Marriage Alive

Remember how you found each other and developed a special relationship before your wedding? You had fun together. You learned to trust and to care for each other as well as to be appropriately intimate in social, emotional, spiritual, intellectual, affectional, and other ways. Hopefully you've followed President Hinckley's counsel when he said: "Choose a companion you can always honor, you can always respect, one who will complement you in your own life, one to whom you can give your entire heart, your entire love, your entire allegiance, your entire loyalty."[22]

We're going to assume that you've done just that! We commend you for that. We also want to reassure you that in these days of marriage woes, when we hear so much about divorce, you have within you the power to make your marriage work. Those who are *committed* to making a marriage last can indeed do so. Viewing marriage as an eternal partnership is the key. Such a perspective on your marriage will bind you together as husband and wife in strong emotional and psychological ways. Add to that the strength of the sealing power of celestial marriage and you have a most powerful relationship.[23] You have all the power you need to make your marriage last as you confront and conquer the inevitable difficulties that will occur.

Your Road to Marriage

As we discussed in chapter 11, marriage can be compared to the two of you mapping the road for your lives and your marriage.

Remember that as you grew up, you developed or created ideas and expectations about marriage. At some point, you began to "see" marriages and become aware of marital roles and responsibilities. For many it was by observing parents or grandparents and realizing the strengths and weaknesses of their marriages. Perhaps it was in school or at church when you began to wonder and think about what it would be like for you to be married. Subtly and directly you were beginning to travel your marital road map.

Then, you began to date. Later you dated more seriously. You met the person whom you are now going to marry or have already married. As you courted and became engaged, you likely changed your ideas of marriage somewhat. "She is better than I thought I'd get!" "He's better than I ever hoped for." As the two of you discussed your plans, you clarified and changed your ideas about marriage, your roles, and your future spouse's roles.

Now the wedding is approaching or has recently occurred. After the wedding you will continue to travel down your road. You will create your road map together as you unitedly make the decisions that lead to the goal of a successful and happy marriage. One of the first decisions you should make is to do what it takes to accomplish that goal. To aid you, we have listed below some ingredients for a happy and successful marriage.

Elements of an Enduring Marriage

There is no one recipe or formula for the right or best marriage, but we suggest that there are a number of characteristics common to most couples as they achieve their greatest marriage potential. Keep in mind that these characteristics apply uniquely to each individual's and couple's personality and situations. One of the great joys in marriage is for each couple to determine and discover how these characteristic ingredients can make their marriage work, and then blend them together to form a beautiful marriage.

Activity in Worship and Church Service

For those of you who are active members of the Church and attend your Church meetings regularly, it may be surprising that the first element of an enduring marriage that we discuss is that of worship and church activity. However, there are many studies and much discussion today that show that shared religious beliefs can be an anchor in the marital relationship.

In many instances worship and Church activity are an important part of courtship and dating. You may recall joyous times of participating in firesides, social events, and other activities. These events were opportunities for you to see one another in a religious context. They were opportunities to join together with other people of similar values.

Often, the participation in worship and church activities gives a couple things to talk about. Thus, in these discussions we find that the couple really gets to know one another. As couples worship together, they gain an insight into each other's beliefs and behaviors related to religious practice.

In marriage, couples find that joining a religious congregation is a means of significant support. Here, people of similar values are able to meet together regularly. Couples establish friendships and can learn about marriage and parenting in formal lessons and in informal discussions and interaction.

A Sense of Humor and Fun

Having fun with your spouse is one of the great benefits of being married. Recall those days and months when you were dating. Both of you put a lot of time and effort into dating and having fun together. You planned well and also responded to the spontaneity of your relationship, and that allowed you to have fun together.

Sometimes, in the business and responsibilities of marriage and parenthood, having fun as a husband and wife disappears. If this happens, it is a tragedy. In fact, in a nationwide random phone survey it was found that having fun was rated as a very important ingredient in happy marriages. The amount of fun that married couples had together emerged as a key factor related to their overall marital happiness.[24] It is true that a good relationship can become even better when you preserve and protect your enjoyable times together.

Having fun together is necessary; it's not just an "optional" aspect of a happy marriage. Authors of another study found that having fun is an essential psychological task in keeping a marriage alive and well.

"To build a happy marriage, couples need to share laughter and humor and to keep interest alive in the relationship. A good marriage is alternately playful and serious, sometimes flirtatious, sometimes difficult and cranky, but always full of life." [25]

SHOWING COMMITMENT TO THE MARRIAGE THROUGH GIVING TIME AND ATTENTION

Commitment to marriage is crucial. Commitment is a decision. Thus, commitment to marriage means that the spouses are dedicated to the idea of being married. They are also committed to being married to each other. As the saying goes, "Pick your mate and make your marriage work."

How is commitment to marriage measured? We have found that the simplest way to assess commitment is to look at the effort, if you will, the time and attention, that is given to it. So, happily married couples find that they give adequate time and attention to one another and to their marriage. This means that they find time in their busy lives to do things together as wife and husband. Time together is a priority and is something that is scheduled and planned for. Spouses do not neglect other responsibilities and commitments, yet they do not neglect marital time either.

In the early months and years of marriage, couples typically spend lots of time together and enjoy one another's company. As the years go by, other responsibilities and commitments come into their lives, which might interfere with "couple time." It is wise counsel from our Church leaders to set aside a night for spending time together each week. If you do this, you will have that time together to look forward to and benefit from weekly togetherness. "Date night," along with the weekly family home evening, give a couple at least two anchor times during the week to connect.

Happily married couples also find time to get away together as a couple. It doesn't matter if these are overnight stays or longer trips. What is important is for a married couple to have time together in a setting that is different from their daily routine. How often should these getaways occur? That is for individual couples to decide. However, keep in mind that the goal is to spend time together and renew the marital relationship as well as to rest and reflect on the blessings and challenges of life. So, these getaways may vary over the years, but it is important that they occur.

More about Romantic Getaways

In order for your relationship to stay healthy, it needs frequent injections of time together and romance. Romantic getaways are a great way to accomplish this. While the family budget includes food, clothing, and shelter, so should the budget include the funds needed to keep the marriage healthy and exciting. While food and shelter sustain life, romantic recharging of the relationship is required to sustain the marriage. All marriages need to be sustained, enriched, and nurtured. If your marriage is not, it will wither and die, as your body would without proper food or water. Even the planning and anticipation of the getaway can increase physical desire for each other and excitement. But don't be afraid to occasionally be spontaneous and take off on getaways that have not been planned.

Husbands, remember that before your wife will feel romantic, she needs to talk and become "reconnected." Allowing for a drive to the getaway location will give her the opportunity to talk as much and as long as she wishes. Make sure you pay attention and are genuinely interested. Be careful not to make things appear like a setup. Be genuinely attentive to your wife's wants and needs, of her as a person with ideas, goals, interests, and feelings. Conversation should center on what you appreciate and love about her. Most importantly, be a good listener. All of life's other problems can wait.

Take time to go shopping or whatever else your wife would like to do on these trips. Often the act of exploring a store with her and reflecting on what she likes and dislikes will help her to shift from being concerned about others to fulfilling her own needs. For her, a little bit of shopping might greatly add to her joy of getting away. You will be surprised how much this will increase her sexual interest. Remember, for your wife, foreplay begins prior to the bedroom.

Good Communication

Good communication is the core of any successful relationship. Generally couples have pretty good communication or they wouldn't have gotten married in the first place! However, it is important to keep in mind that effective communication is a skill. Like all skills, communication can be improved and enhanced. Also, the skills of communication can dwindle if not practiced. Therefore, couples need to work at good communication. Many happy couples find that books, magazine articles such as those found in the *Ensign*, and similar sources are useful, helpful, and even fun to read and apply.

One approach that can be helpful in continually improving marital communication is captured in the three letters, L-U-V. *L* stands for listening. *U* stands for understanding. *V* stands for validating.

Listening. When you are in conversation with your partner, do you really listen (L) to him or her? We convey listening by simple things. Do you have appropriate eye contact and pay attention to what the other person is saying? Or are you reading a newspaper or magazine or perhaps watching television? Put down the paper and pay attention!

Understanding. When you are in a conversation with your partner, do you understand (U) him or her? Understanding is important for both the speaker and the listener. Do you really care what the other person thinks or is saying? Do you really care about how the other person feels? Are you attempting to understand what the other person is saying? The key here is to understand what is being said while not necessarily agreeing. Understanding is communicated by simple gestures such as eye contact, nodding your head in agreement, saying such things as, "Uh-huh, yes, okay," or "I understand." It can also be helpful to ask a simple question such as, "Tell me if I'm getting this right," or "I heard you say that . . ." If such simple things are used to communicate, not only can the listener make sure that he or she understands, but the speaker can also correct what he or she is trying to say.

Validating. This sort of conversation, listening and understanding, sets up the final ingredient for good communication, that is, to be validated (V). For the speaker, being validated means that he or she has been listened to and understood. Feeling understood engenders feelings of respect, importance, and self-worth. For the listener, validating produces the knowledge that he or she did understand what feelings, thoughts, or intentions the other person was communicating. What can be more important than to feel respected and understood—validated—in a conversation? This is particularly true when communicating with our spouse with whom we have a loving and meaningful relationship.

Remember that good communication is a skill that can be enhanced and improved by everyone. There is some truth to the idea that as married couples live together over time they may tend to take each other for granted in certain ways. So, make sure that in your marriage you are doing little things continually so that your communication stays clear and even improves. Practice "L-U-Ving" in your relationship!

Flexibility

Finally, flexibility is essential to an enduring marriage. Happily married couples are willing to make adjustments in their marriage. Going into marriage, husbands and wives often have different expectations about what each partner should do in a marriage. Successful couples work as a team and share in the planning of their marital and family roles and responsibilities. Then when circumstances change or unexpected events require a change of plans, they adapt and help each other out.

For example, this may require one spouse doing a larger portion of the housework than originally planned if his or her partner suddenly becomes very busy with a new Church calling. Couples also need to be flexible in other areas such as how they handle the finances, how they spend their time socially, and of course in their sexual relationship. If both partners are willing to adjust their individual preferences and actions for the benefit of the couple and the family, they will have less conflict and greater harmony in their marriage.

Our Best Wishes to You

We've covered a lot of information in this book. Remember, our goal has been to provide information and ideas that you might discuss and apply to your marriage. Of course, there's a significant amount of additional information that we couldn't present here because of limited space. Such information is available to you from many sources, including professionals, Church leaders, books, and other resources. As you have questions, never fail to seek answers *as a couple.* We wish you eternal happiness in your marriage.

References:

1. Brent A. Barlow, "Procreation," *Encyclopedia of Mormonism*, 5 vols. ed. Daniel H. Ludlow (New York: Macmillan, 1992), s.v. "procreation."
2. Edward L. Kimball, ed. *The Teachings of Spencer W. Kimball* (Salt Lake City: Bookcraft, 1982), 305–306.
3. Linda J. Waite and Maggie Gallagher, *The Case for Marriage* (New York: Doubleday, 2000), 13–35.
4. Spencer W. Kimball, "Thoughts on Marriage Compatibility," *Ensign,* Sept. 1981, 45.
5. David R. Mace, *Success in Marriage* (Abingdon: Nashville, 1958), 47–48.
6. Kimball, "Thoughts on Marriage Compatibility," 45.
7. Edward O. Laumann, et al., *The Social Organizational of Sexuality: Sexual Practices in the United States* (Chicago: The University of Chicago Press, 1994), 374–375; Waite and Gallagher, *The Case for Marriage*, 47–64.
8. William Masters, and Virginia Johnson, and Robert C. Kolodny, *Human Sexuality, 4th ed.*(New York: Harper Collins, 1992), 71–86.
9. Lindsay R. Curtis, *Sensible Sex: A Guide for Newlyweds* (Deseret Book, 1997), 35.
10. Helen Singer Kaplan, *The New Sex Therapy* (New York: Brunner/Mazel, 1974), 523–524.
11. Masters, Johnson, and Kolodny, *Human Sexuality*, 71–86.
12. Rosemary Basson, "Female Sexual Response: The Role of Drugs in the Management of Sexual Dysfunction," *Obstetrics and Gynecology*, 98, no. 2 (2001): 350–53.
13. Marie N. Robinson, *The Power of Sexual Surrender* (New York: Doubleday, 1959), 75–76.
14. Robert F. Stahmann and William J. Hiebert, *Premarital and Remarital Counseling: The Professional's Handbook* (San Francisco: Jossey-Bass, 1997), 3–5.
15. Waite and Gallagher, *The Case for Marriage*, 65–77.
16. Kimball, "Thoughts on Marriage Compatibility," 45.
17. Laumann, et al., *The Social Organizational of Sexuality: Sexual Practices in the United States*, 340.
18. Kimball, ed., *The Teachings of Spencer W. Kimball*, 302.
19. Laumann, et al., *The Social Organizational of Sexuality: Sexual Practices in the United States*, 86–93.

20. Robert F. Stahmann, "Reflections on Traveling the Road to Marriage," *Marriage and Families*, Jan. 2003, 9–13.

21. RELATE was developed by the Marriage Study Consortium at Brigham Young University. Founded in 1979, the Marriage Study Consortium is a nonprofit organization with the specific tasks of developing research and outreach tools that can be used directly with the public and that can be used to gather information about relationships. The consortium consists of a group of scholars, researchers, family life educators, and counselors from varied religious and educational backgrounds who are dedicated to strengthening and understanding premarital and marital relationships. To take RELATE or for further information, log on to www.relate-institute.org or phone at 801-422-4359 or e-mail at relate@byu.edu.

22. Gordon B. Hinckley, "Life's Expectations," *Ensign,* Feb. 1999, 2.

23. Thomas B. Holman, Jeffry H. Larson, and Robert F. Stahmann, "Preparing for an Eternal Marriage," *Strengthening Our Families: An In-Depth Look at the Proclamation on the Family,* ed. David C. Dollahite (Salt Lake City: Deseret Book, 2000).

24. Scott Stanley, Daniel Trathen, Savanna McCain, and Milt Bryan, *A Lasting Promise: A Christian Guide to Fighting for Your Marriage* (San Francisco: Jossey-Bass, 1998), 236.

25. Judith S. Wallerstein and Sandra Blakeslee, *The Good Marriage: How and Why Love Lasts* (Boston: Houghton Mifflin, 1995), 332.